D0844890

THE THEORY OF
SOCIAL ACTION

Studies in Phenomenology and
Existential Philosophy

GENERAL EDITOR
JAMES M. EDIE

CONSULTING EDITORS

David Carr
Edward S. Casey
Stanley Cavell
Roderick M. Chisholm
Hubert L. Dreyfus
William Earle
J. N. Findlay
Dagfinn Føllesdal
Marjorie Grene
Dieter Henrich
Emmanuel Levinas
Alphonso Lingis

William L. McBride
J. N. Mohanty
Maurice Natanson
Frederick Olafson
Paul Ricoeur
George Schrader
Calvin O. Schrag
Robert Sokolowski
Herbert Spiegelberg
Charles Taylor
Samuel J. Todes
Bruce W. Wilshire

The Correspondence of
Alfred Schutz and Talcott Parsons

THE THEORY OF
SOCIAL ACTION

Edited by Richard Grathoff

INDIANA UNIVERSITY PRESS
Bloomington and London

H
61
.S443
1977

Copyright © 1978 by Richard Grathoff

All rights reserved

No part of this book may be reproduced or utilized in any form
or by any means, electronic or mechanical, including photocopying
and recording, or by any information storage and retrieval system,
without permission in writing from the publisher. The Association
of American University Presses' Resolution on Permissions constitutes
the only exception to this prohibition.

Manufactured in the United States of America

Library of Congress Cataloging in Publication Data
Schutz, Alfred, 1899–1959.
The theory of social action.
(Studies in phenomenology and existential
philosophy)
Includes bibliographical references and index.
1. Social sciences—Methodology. 2. Schutz,
Alfred, 1899–1959. 3. Parsons, Talcott, 1902–
I. Parsons, Talcott, 1902–   joint author.
II. Grathoff, Richard H., 1934–   III. Title.
H61.S443   1978   300'.1'8   77-15761
ISBN 0-253-35957-0   1 2 3 4 5 82 81 80 79 78

MAR 2 4 1981

CONTENTS

FOREWORD

Soon after I came to the Graduate Faculty of the New School for Social Research in 1951 to study with Alfred Schutz, he told me about his meetings and correspondence with Talcott Parsons. It was only in recent years, however, that I had an opportunity to read the manuscripts from which this book is drawn. Although the past twenty-five years have brought forth significant contributions to the literature of the theory and methodology of the social sciences, I am left with the impression that the themes of the Schutz–Parsons correspondence are still vital to an understanding of the logical foundations of social science. To be sure, the correspondence focuses on a sociological debate, which is carried on by two remarkable social scientists. Readers may legitimately find in the exchange further insight into the positions of Schutz and Parsons as well as valuable suggestions regarding the thought of Max Weber and others. No doubt, readers will also find interesting analyses of the substantive points on which Schutz and Parsons disagree and, occasionally, concur. For some, this correspondence will have predominantly historical interest; they may think that the issues under consideration have been absorbed and transformed by more recent developments in the social sciences but that it is important to respect the sources of sociological thought. My own view of the correspondence is that its dominant albeit reluctant theme is the relationship between philosophy and social science. Such an interpretation demands not only explanation but defense.

Early in Schutz's discussion of Parsons' *The Structure of Social Action,* he says that Parsons' "purpose is to demonstrate that the four men in question [Marshall, Pareto, Durkheim, and Weber], though of different nationalities, different social origin, different education, and different attitudes toward their science, nevertheless converge, in all essentials, upon certain fundamental postu-

lates of the methodology and epistemology of the social sciences."
And later, in summarizing what he takes to be the "many great
merits" of Parsons' work, Schutz tells us that

> they consist, first of all, in the attempt to build up a basic methodology
> of the social sciences by starting from the question: what do the great
> masters of sociology really do in performing their concrete research
> work? Secondly, the attempt is made to unify their methodological
> remarks into a great system of theory, the theory of action, and to
> outline the constructive elements of such a theory as well as the
> implications which arise both from the historical background of the
> social sciences and from their logical structure.

He goes on, then, to regret "that Professor Parsons intentionally
renounces the examination of the logical and philosophical foundations upon which a correct methodology of the social sciences
must be based." Parsons replies:

> we seem to be unable to have a satisfactory meeting of minds because
> our foci of interest in these problems are quite different. I found myself
> marking at a number of points statements of yours which imply that
> my book was, along with the secondary examination of the work of
> other people, primarily a study of the methodology and epistemology
> of social science. On the very first page of your manuscript you refer
> ... to my purpose of demonstrating that the four men converged on
> certain fundamental postulates of this methodology and epistemology.
> This statement seems to me symptomatic of a point of view which runs
> throughout your treatment. I think it is fair to say that you never
> carefully and systematically consider these problems in terms of their
> relation to a generalized system of *scientific theory*. It is this, not
> methodology and epistemology, which was quite definitely the central
> focus of my own interest.

The quotations just given are representative of the encounter
between the two thinkers. Much of the essential vocabulary of the
discussion is understood by each man in a fundamentally different way: not only "methodology" but also "theory" is necessarily
philosophical for Schutz; Parsons understands his work to be concerned with problems of a primarily scientific rather than philosophical character. I am not suggesting that terminological
confusions on both sides account for the failure of the discussion
to be joined. To the contrary, it is philosophical matters which

explain the confusion in language. Parsons is explicit about
Schutz's philosophical orientation:

> at a great many points you are interested in certain ranges of philo-
> sophical problems for their own sake which, quite self-consciously and
> with specific methodological justification, I have not treated. You are,
> for instance, continually attempting to point out certain things about
> what the subjective processes of action really are in what must be
> taken as a directly ontological sense. At another point you speak of the
> problem of ultimate value, again in a strictly philosophical sense. It
> is, I think, a corollary of my concentration of interest on a system of
> theory that I have attempted to minimize discussion of, and commit-
> ment to positions on, this philosophical level as much as possible.

But to say that methodology and theory are philosophical, for
Schutz, does not mean that in his view a sociologist must become
an epistemologist. Neither does it mean that Parsons is not entitled to limit the scope of his inquiry. The terminological problem
is merely the tip of a philosophical iceberg.

Late in the correspondence, Schutz writes: "I realized immediately the importance and the value of your system and also the
fact that it starts exactly where my own book ends." A full account of the meaning of the last part of that statement would
provide the beginnings of an explanation of Schutz's conception
of the relationship between social science and philosophy; in turn,
such an account would explain the reasons for Schutz's conviction
that Parsons' work was important, valuable, and open to philosophical grounding in terms of an approach which Schutz had
tried to provide in *Der sinnhafte Aufbau der sozialen Welt.* Very
briefly, Schutz believed that most often social scientists are, philosophically speaking, "naive realists," that is, they begin analysis
by taking for granted the epistemic status of the common-sense
world within which their professional problems arise. In phenomenological terms, most social scientists remain within the "natural attitude" in which the "world" of "social world" is untroubled
by philosophical doubts. It is hardly the case for Schutz that naive
realism is primordial sin! The sociologist is fully entitled to enter
into sociological work which is not philosophically grounded. But
the price exacted for such entrance is that the fundamental terms
of sociological discourse are tacitly affected by the epistemological
implications of naive realism. The philosopher's work consists in
the radical clarification of the conditions necessary for the possi-

bility of the "world" explored by the social scientist. The sociologist begins where the philosopher ends.

Does this mean that Schutz thought Parsons was a naive realist? Does not Parsons maintain that he is indebted to a neo-Kantian position? And is philosophical naiveté always on the side of realism? Can there be a naive transcendentalism? It might appear that these questions are quite marginal to the central issues of the correspondence. In fact, they bring us to what is perhaps its most bitterly ironic moment. Schutz does not say that Parsons is a naive realist; he does say that Parsons' system is philosophically naive in its "identification of *scientific* knowledge and *scientific* logic as such with the rational element of action. . . ." Now the context of that remark is a discussion of scientific knowledge. Schutz tries to contrast the concepts and judgments of the scientist with those of the actor in daily life. There is, Schutz points out, a "modified logic of daily life" which is appropriate for the analysis of the partial knowledge which the ordinary actor has of the empirical world. Husserl's inquiries have provided the clue to a "modified logic." But in order to follow that clue, it is necessary to reorient oneself from the stance of the empirical scientist to that of the "critical" philosopher. Very simply, Schutz is drawing on Kant's distinction between "naive" and "critical" philosophy: the former begins inquiry with the object of knowledge; the latter turns to the conditions for the possibility of knowledge. Indeed, Kant's philosophy is known as the "critical philosophy." And here is the root of the misunderstanding between Schutz, who meant "philosophically naive" in a neutral sense, and Parsons, who took that expression to be pejorative.

Parsons writes:

> My insistence on the continuity of the basic categories of logic and observation on the one hand in the most sophisticated science, on the other hand in the most simple common-sense action, is fundamental to my whole position. You state that this is a philosophically naive identification. That is your opinion. I find nothing in your argument to shake my position. I can assure you that I have thought it through exceedingly carefully from a great many different points of view and though it is possible that it is wrong, I think that I can say with considerable confidence that it is not naive.

One can hear the death knell of the correspondence in these words. Curiously enough, the trouble concerning what is "philosophically naive" comes soon after Schutz writes, "I agree fully with Professor Parsons that the positivistic ideal of scientifically valid knowledge is insufficient for the explanation of human acts." It may be that underlying sources of disagreement between the two thinkers derive, in part, from what appears to unite them. In philosophy, neo-Kantianism has served as a friendly neighbor to phenomenology: Natorp and Cassirer, at least, shared a universe of discourse with Husserl. In fact, Schutz once told me that he started his philosophical life as a neo-Kantian. Labels have their limits. I would judge from the correspondence not only that each man understood an implicit neo-Kantianism in a somewhat different way but that each man stressed a different aspect of "science" in neo-Kantianism. In any case, phenomenology was of no help to the discussion.

From his references to phenomenology in the correspondence, it seems that Parsons thinks of it in metaphysical or ontological terms. He writes:

> We may now come to the question of the objective and subjective points of view. I really think that I have finally succeeded in straightening out the difference between us on this question. I think what you mean essentially is an ontological reality, what a concrete real actor "really" experiences. I think I have legitimate reasons to be skeptical that by your analysis or by any others available it is possible to arrive at anything approaching a definitive description of such a reality. I am afraid I must confess to being skeptical of phenomenological analysis.

Here the distance between what Schutz understands as phenomenology and what Parsons takes it to be is so vast that productive discussion is precluded on both sides. Although Parsons had listed *Der sinnhafte Aufbau der sozialen Welt* in the bibliography of *The Structure of Social Action* and has some references to Husserl's *Logische Untersuchungen* in the final chapter, phenomenology remains largely out of reach. If neo-Kantianism failed to bring Schutz and Parsons together, phenomenology would hardly succeed. Yet phenomenology haunts the correspondence as an uninvitable guest. A few years after the abortive end of the correspondence, when Schutz began teaching at the New School for Social Research, Alvin Johnson, its distinguished president, gave him some friendly advice (so Schutz told me): "Don't try to teach our students phenomenology; they won't take it!" That advice was accepted. Instead of adopting the language of Husserl,

Schutz presented his ideas in the context of the writings of James, Dewey, Whitehead, Mead, Cooley, and Thomas. Perhaps his experience with Parsons was a factor in his heeding of Johnson's warning.

If a profoundly shared interest in Weber and the Continental tradition in sociology did not suffice to unite Schutz and Parsons, if a common concern with neo-Kantianism did not bring them together, and if phenomenology was intrinsically unsuited to overcome the philosophical differences between the two thinkers, then it may seem that the mutual dissatisfaction which is so much a part of the correspondence was the inevitable result of mismated minds trying to come to terms with each other. I do not think that this is a fair appraisal, nor have I meant to emphasize disagreement at the expense of some positive features of the correspondence. Despite serious differences in interpretation, both men are deeply concerned with the theory of social action, with the status of the subjective interpretation of meaning, with the relationship between common-sense and scientific constructs of social reality, with the problem of rationality in human action, and, despite everything which divides them, with the meaning of theory in social science. Why then did the discussion fail? Parsons himself offers one answer. He writes:

> Just as I have charged you with failure to understand *my* position adequately, it is quite possible that the principal source of the difficulty lies in *my* failure to understand *you*. I think I have given sufficient evidence ... that this cannot be the whole story, but it may well be an important part of it; but if it is, there is still the further problem of whether on the one hand I have simply failed to understand a philosophical approach which is really concerned with quite different problems from mine, and on the whole, instead of criticizing each other we have simply been talking about different things.

Parsons' speculation does not, in my judgment, provide a way out of the impasse. What divides the two men is not different philosophies concerned with different problems but rather the meaning of philosophy for social science. For Schutz, sociology cannot ground itself; epistemology is not a luxury but a necessity for the social scientist. Nor, from a phenomenological perspective, can science, if it is to be truly rigorous, provide its own conceptual foundation. For Parsons, the demand is for demarcating science and philosophy, for allowing philosophy to enter the discussion only when it is needed. It would seem that philosophy should speak only when spoken to! Yet Parsons is immersed in philosophical issues. The discussion in the correspondence of the status of "fact" emerges, I think, because Parsons' utilization of the notion of a conceptual "scheme" is philosophically internal to his sociological position, not simply because Schutz understands "fact" in a different way. Even here, the correspondents fail to meet each other. In his retrospective statement for this volume, Parsons has very usefully turned to developments in his thought which postdate the correspondence. In the same spirit, I bring to the reader's attention a passage in an essay by Schutz which was published in 1953:

> All our knowledge of the world, in common-sense as well as in scientific thinking, involves constructs, i.e., a set of abstractions, generalizations, formalizations, idealizations specific to the respective level of thought organization. Strictly speaking, there are no such things as facts, pure and simple. All facts are from the outset facts selected from a universal context by the activities of our mind. They are, therefore, always interpreted facts, either looked at as detached from their context by an artificial abstraction or facts considered in their particular setting. In either case, they carry along their interpretational inner and outer horizon. This does not mean that, in daily life or in science, we are unable to grasp the reality of the world. It just means that we grasp merely certain aspects of it, namely those which are relevant to us either for carrying on our business of living or from the point of view of a body of accepted rules of procedure of thinking called the method of science. (*Collected Papers,* vol. 1, p. 5)

Schutz's philosophical position in 1953 was in no way significantly different from what he stood for in 1940. The quotation is phenomenological through and through. Nor is it a formulation unique to one essay. It does represent, I think, a philosophical view of "fact" which embraces the notion of "scheme" and indicates what a phenomenological approach to "fact" might yield: something fundamental to social science which Schutz and Parsons have in common. If there is any merit to this suggestion, then it points to a genuine encounter which could have taken place, provided that philosophy and sociology are viewed as intimately related to each other, as needing and deserving each other. Sociologists as social scientists are not required to do philosophical work, nor are philosophers assigned the task of doing empirical research. Both sides have a certain autonomy, but final sovereignty rests with the integrity of knowledge. If Parsons begins where Schutz ends, it is still possible to bring beginning and end together, not by an artificial synthesis but through integral reflection. In taking leave of the correspondence, let us give the final word, for the moment, to Merleau-Ponty: "The sociologist philosophizes every time he is required not only to record but to comprehend the facts. At the moment of interpretation, he is himself already a philosopher."

Maurice Natanson

INTRODUCTION

The Schutz–Parsons correspondence recalls the times of the approach of World War II, the aftermath of the Great Depression, and the exodus of European social scientists to the United States. In such times rationality and social order seem to fade into the papers and files of mere academic debate. It was either late in 1938 or in the spring of the following year that Professor F. A. Hayek, then editor of *Economica* at the London School of Economics, invited Alfred Schutz to write a review of Talcott Parsons' *The Structure of Social Action* (New York and London: McGraw-Hill, 1937). Though Schutz accepted, he was never himself to publish his essay and critique of Parsons.

In a way, therefore, this little volume is a late answer to Hayek's invitation. It traces the full course of discussions between the immigrant Viennese scholar, who was just settling with his family in New York, and the social theorist from Harvard. The reader will find himself engaged in an intense, sometimes stormy, and, at places, embittered exchange of notes and letters, which leads into a rather poignant debate on the differences between phenomenological and structural–functional analyses.

The heretofore published writings of both men give no hint of their heavy discourse. They decided to keep it a private affair. Parsons, to the knowledge of this editor, never quoted or referred to Schutz in his published writings. Schutz kept his silence, which he offered to Parsons in a final letter on March 17, 1941. His occasional references to

Talcott Parsons, for instance in his *Collected Papers* (The Hague: Nijhoff, 1962–66), reflect his continuous respect for a theory of social action, which Schutz had also thought to advance.

Late in 1969, ten years after her husband's early death, Mrs. Ilse Schutz turned to Professor Parsons for his opinion. Students of Schutz, especially the editors of his *Collected Papers,* being familiar with his unpublished writings, had proposed publication of this correspondence. Mrs. Schutz had been hesitant. Several years passed, but then Professor Parsons encouraged her and gave his consent for publication in a letter to Mrs. Schutz (July 23, 1971):

> I would see no objection to having these materials published if you so desire. I know from his own letter which closed the correspondence that Dr. Schutz felt that I had misinterpreted his intentions. I very much appreciated the positive things which he did in fact say about my work, but it did seem to me for the immediate purposes at the time that it was justified in my comments to concentrate on the points of difference which, as I said earlier in this letter, were both real and serious. It may well be that I was unduly defensive in my attitude. Perhaps because I have felt that my book, *The Structure of Social Action,* had been unfairly criticized in a number of different quarters and perhaps I was especially sensitive to critique coming from the German language culture in which through my work on Max Weber I had become immersed.

I had just finished translating the first volume of the *Collected Papers* into Schutz's native language when Mrs. Schutz asked me to prepare these materials for print. I proposed a three-part division of the papers, which required different forms of editing. Part I, the Schutzean essay on Parsons' *Theory of Social Action* and originally planned as the review for *Economica,* has been edited with respect only to style and sentence structure. It contains some passages which have already been published under a separate title ("The Social World and the Theory of Social Action," *Coll.*

Pap. 2, pp. 3–19). It may serve the interested reader as a basis to compare both editions. Its earlier editor, Arvid Broderson, had decided against any editorial changes. I adopted his rather conservative attitude in my dealing with the Schutz–Parsons letters (part II): only a few paragraphs and letter headings have been introduced to facilitate the reader's orientation.

The main exchange between Parsons and Schutz lasted only three months and was broken off in April 1941. Nothing is known to me about later meetings between the two men. Most likely they referred critically to each other's respective positions in their lectures and seminars.

This raises a subtle problem with respect to our contemporary understanding of that particular debate. Only one of the authors could be asked for a retrospective view. I am especially grateful for the understanding of Mrs. Schutz and her support in this respect. To Professor Parsons my sincere thanks for his willingness to write such a retrospect for this volume. Slightly edited, with his consent, it has been incorporated into part III.

The discussions of social action presented in this book focus on four of the most problematic issues in all sociological inquiry. They can each be called upon in just a few words. As problems, they are easy to grasp even by a beginner, but they lead quickly into extreme difficulties. Each of these issues throws its own divisive shadow through contemporary scholarly debate. Unfortunately, however, such divisions are often taken as an invitation to choose sides, too often through rejection of one position rather than an understanding of the other. However, careful reading of the following debate between Alfred Schutz and Talcott Parsons may also lead the more mature student not simply to add fuel to his or her earlier opinions, but to pursue the issue and deepen one's perception of this delicate and most precarious texture of social life: the structure of social action.

The *first issue* of the Schutz–Parsons debate refers back
to Max Weber's incipient formulation of a sociology of action and could be called the *Weberian Suggestion.* It has
been first of all Max Weber who conceived sociology as a
rigorous scientific field of research that should always relate back to the contexts of human interaction. When people interact they cut their paths through the historical and
biographical thickets of the social world; they suffer or tol-
erate Others in pursuing their own ends; they may also
abstain from acting; perhaps they inhibit Others in pursuing their own course. Men's actions are thus oriented to
their fellow men, to their motives and intentions. A study
of social action has to grasp such meanings of action as
intended by the actors, and it has to relate that subjective
meaning to the various historical objectivations in a social
situation, say, to a science or some tradition, to a world of
ideas. This is the problem: Would it not be possible, Weber
suggests, to give sociology a solid foundation by starting
from some methodology that could grasp this texture of
social action? While Weber, however, kept his suggestion
closely related to a historical understanding of social structures, both Schutz and Parsons pursued this foundational
problem somewhat differently: Schutz followed the Weberian suggestion into a study of social action as being
founded in the common-sense structures of everyday life;
Parsons proposed his "Theory of Social Action" in order to
formulate such a foundation.[1]

The reader must trace this apparent diversion in following Weber's suggestion throughout the Schutz–Parsons debate. But he or she should be immediately prepared to
encounter a *second issue* that goes back to René Descartes'
first conception for any such study of human conscience,
consciousness, and understanding: It has often been called
the *Cartesian Dilemma.*[2] Every study of interaction and of
the mutual understanding of one's own self and that of
others, every theory of action that relates back to the actors'
mutual orientation, their motives and intentions, must face
this basic problem: How can we at all reach the subjectivity

of the Other in its givenness among the other objects of the
world when we cannot avoid starting from the subjectivity
of our own perceiving and judging? How could this problem
of intersubjectivity be solved? Is it at all possible to con-
struct an objective social science in starting from subjective
experience structures?[3]

The *third issue* behind the Schutz–Parsons debate is a
Kantian Problem. It is explicitly mentioned by Talcott Parsons in his retrospect to this volume.[4] Briefly, this is the
frame of that problem: Kant's conception of human understanding separated rather sharply the human mind from
the world of the senses in their sensual and living fullness
of immediacy. Hence, Kant had to ask how it is at all possible that men's perceiving, cognitive constructing, and experiencing can reach the world as an empirical world of vivid
creatures. Kant proposes that this can be achieved by the
application of what he called "schemata" of understanding.
Such schemata as the human mind acquires are its means
to reach the world of objects as objects known. All concepts
of thought require such schemata in order to become applicable and thus relational to their respective thought-
objects. However, the origin and constitution of these
schemata remain an open problem, which Kant refers to as
a secret of the human soul.[5] This question becomes especially urgent when applied to what is perhaps the most
central sociological theme: Can our perceiving and dealing,
our acting and reacting with the Other as our fellowman be
conceived in terms of such schemata?[6]

Finally, the *fourth issue* of the Schutz–Parsons debate,
which needs the most acute attention of the reader, is of
unique concern for both theoreticians. This is an issue of
their own. They start discussing the problem of rationality
in the social world and reach a dividing point, which they
were unable to bridge: It may be called the *Schutz–Parsons
Divide.* They discuss the eternal problems of social order, to
what extent a social world may be manageable by reason
and understanding, to what extent rationality could be part
of social life. Of course, the question most likely troubled

man when he first perceived his fellowman as somehow in line with and similar to himself. As mentioned before, Parsons had invited several colleagues at Harvard for a seminar on this topic. Schutz entered this debate with a troubling suggestion: The rationality of the social world, he admits, as formulated by Max Weber and then interpreted by Talcott Parsons, is, of course, intrinsic to sociological theory and all social sciences. However, this rationality must always be alien to and distinct from everyday life. A scientific enterprise is never simply a part, but always a distinct partition of everyday life and its discourse. Hence, sociological interest in the rationality of the social world must start, according to Schutz, from an analysis of the concrete structures of our experiencing everyday life. Parsons, on the other hand, considered this proposal as irrelevant for his own inquiry. This basic difference remains at the core of the Schutz–Parsons debate.

This introduction must be limited to a reconstruction of some features of the Schutz–Parsons debate of the early 1940s. To go beyond the outlining of major issues, to contemplate, for instance, the motives of both authors to refrain from a public dispute of their differences, or to analyze perhaps even the consequences of this "blackout" for the methodological discussions during the intervening years between phenomenological and structural–functional positions would interfere with what I decided had to be a very restricted editorial role. Any attempt, for instance, to pursue the consequences of this debate for the subsequent formation of Parsons' as well as Schutz's own theories, which the informed reader will immediately become aware of while following their exchange in this book, needs a most careful elaboration not appropriate here. The scene of their debate is clearly defined by their own publications and the reaction of the scientific community at that time. Alfred Schutz's book *Der sinnhafte Aufbau der sozialen Welt (The Phenomenology of the Social World)* had appeared in Vienna in 1932 and had come to the attention of English readers through a review in *Economica* in 1937. Talcott

Parsons' first book, *The Structure of Social Action,* was published the same year. Both works received the immediate attention of the scholarly public, however with mixed reactions. These can be easily retraced by the interested reader.[7]

Our present concern is the mutual perception of the two men, which apparently differed from the very beginning. Parsons recalled later in a letter to Schutz: "I remember about 1937 having a rather long conversation with Schelting about [your book] and saying essentially that I could not see that for the purposes of my treatment of Max Weber, for instance, it was necessary to go into the kind of analysis of the subjective point of view in relation to the time element which was the central theme of your analysis."[8] Their interest in each other's work focused on the problem of time in social action. But while Parsons thought he could circumvent this question, Schutz pushed it into the foreground. He had read *The Structure of Social Action* soon after its publication. In his first essay published after his emigration to the United States Schutz praised Parsons' Weber study as "an excellent presentation of his theory"; and an earlier working paper, which outlines the significance of phenomenological methods for the social sciences, stated explicitly his objective: "Application of Husserl's time analyses toward the 'Structure of Social Action' as being understood by Weber and Parsons."[9] Schutz was working on the review of Parsons' book for *Economica* that Hayek had asked him to prepare. He looked forward to discussing this review with Parsons before publishing it.

Their first personal meeting should have taken place in early September 1939, during the annual meeting of the American Sociological Society in Boston. But the outbreak of the war in Europe forced Schutz to return to his New York office before they could meet. Both corresponded during the following months. Parsons invited Schutz to come to Harvard, Schutz extended his invitation to see Parsons in New York. They finally met in Harvard on April 13, 1940, where Parsons had invited Schutz to read a paper on "Rationality and the Structure of the Social World."[10]

This Harvard Seminar on Rationality had been organized jointly by Talcott Parsons and Joseph Schumpeter during the academic year of 1939–40. It seems Parsons had already presented his own paper in the winter term: "An Approach to the Analysis of the Role of Rationality in Social Action," a summary of his position detailed in *The Structure of Social Action*.[11] It contains neither a reference to Schutz nor to his theoretical position.

Schutz, on the other hand, went into an extensive discussion of Parsons' position. His paper elaborated the problem of rationality toward the four main issues mentioned above. Even in his opening statement, Schutz tried to establish a basic line of understanding with Talcott Parsons:

> The thesis I want to defend is the following: *Rationality* in its strict meaning is a category of the *scientific observation* of the social world and not a category in the mind of the *actor within* the social world. The conceptual scheme of rationality is, therefore, valid in its primary denotation only on the level of *theoretical* observation; to other levels of our experience of the social world, it is applicable in a modified and restricted meaning only. What in general must be understood by *"rational action"* can best be characterized by reproducing the definition Professor Parsons gives in his most remarkable study *The Structure of Social Action:* "Action is rational in so far as it pursues ends possible within the conditions of the situation, and by the means which, among those available to the actor, are intrinsically best adapted to the end for reasons understandable and verifiable by positive empirical science."[12]

Talcott Parsons responded sharply to Schutz's presentation. He felt he was being attacked. As quoted above, he felt especially sensitive about critique from European quarters: Having been at the University of Heidelberg, where he also had received his doctorate, he felt himself to be part of that Weberian milieu. He might have been further annoyed, perhaps, by the still uncertain linguistic competence of the emigrant, taking statements too literally and as being addressed toward him in a manner Schutz never intended. For instance, the original manuscript for the Schutz lecture contains this passage not directed at Parsons, but easily misunderstood:

> I have no intention at all of sharing the presumptiousness of certain methodologists in criticizing what is performed with true and real workmanship in the social sciences. One of the greatest methodologists, Max Weber, formed this adage: "I hate the permanent sharpening of methodological knives if there is nothing on the table to be carved." The role of methodology is more humble.

The Schutzean phrase sounds too much like some of the more repugnant lines Talcott Parsons was used to during those years. Schutz apparently quite clearly felt Parsons' rejection. It must have deeply hurt the man whose only intention had been to establish a dialogue with a scholar of whose work he thought highly. Schutz went through his Harvard paper on rationality again, at the same time working on the long and detailed critical review of Parsons' *Structure of Social Action* for *Economica*. But while Schutz was writing these essays, Parsons had proceeded to a new text, some "larger manuscript" that he sent Schutz, asking for his opinion. Hence, their exchange of letters and finally Schutz's mailing of his review article to Parsons were already accompanied by a considerable misunderstanding on both sides as to which of their papers each of them meant when referring to each other. The stage was set for more than just conceptual misunderstandings when they finally exchanged the following letters in late fall of 1940.[13]

One word concerning the material itself: all letters were typewritten. Parsons used Harvard stationery; Schutz wrote on his private stationery. The correspondence started in late summer 1939. The initial letters, however, attempt only to arrange dates and exchange notices or greetings. Being of minor interest, they have been excluded. With one exception all letters were written in English. Only the first letter of Schutz in this volume had to be translated; he had written it in German. It was mailed, together with his essay, to Parsons in November 1940. With an introductory letter from Talcott Parsons, it forms the main part of part I.

Nearly forty years have passed since Professor Hayek's invitation to Alfred Schutz. I wish to thank, also in the name of Mrs. Schutz, all scholars and friends who assisted this publication on its adventurous path. In particular I would like to mention James Edie, who helped the volume over some difficult hurdles. My special thanks go to Maurice Natanson for editorial and other advice. I want to thank Gordon Turpin, now back in his native Canada, for his help with translations. Much credit for this edition belongs to my friend Walter Sprondel, with whom I spent many an hour going over problems as they arose. He is now preparing a German edition (Frankfurt: Suhrkamp Verlag), which is to appear at about the same time as this edition. The closing word, however, goes to that person without whom this volume would not have been possible at all. The reader, I am sure, will honor her decision to publish this correspondence. My deepest respect to Mrs. Ilse Schutz for her patience and encouragement. I bear the responsibility for all faults this edition still has.

Richard Grathoff

PART I

Inquiry into the
Structure of Social Action

Cambridge, October 30, 1940

Dear Dr. Schutz:

I was very sorry to hear from Winternitz, who called me up the other day, that you have been seriously ill. At least I am very glad that you are better now, and I hope that you will soon be fully recovered.

I had wondered a little why I had not heard from you with regard to the manuscript I sent to you, but there has been, of course, no hurry about it. He tells me, however, that you have written a commentary on it, and I shall be greatly interested to see it any time that you are able to send it to me. Perhaps rather than returning the manuscript to me you would be kind enough to send it to Dr. Voegelin at the University of Alabama. I promised that I would send him a copy as soon as one was available, and when you are through with this one it would save trouble all around to have you send it direct to him.

Our group on Rationality is not meeting this fall, but Professor Schumpeter and I are trying to assemble a group of manuscripts so that we can see how close they come to forming a publishable volume. We will let you know as soon as we have enough of them to form any sort of a judgment.

With sincere regards,
Talcott Parsons

New York, November 15, 1940

Dear Professor Parsons:

Thank you for your kind lines of 30th October. No one regrets more than I that I had to let so much time pass before writing again. Partly responsible was my illness, about which my friend Winternitz informed you. On the other hand, I had hoped to be able to provide you with my position regarding your theories, promised in April, much earlier than is now the case. I can, however, honestly say that, in spite of some serious obstacles and regrettable interruptions, I have devoted the little time that professional demands have left me to a thorough restudying of your book and your short manuscript on rationality.

In scientific matters I am by nature a slow worker who is given to lengthy consideration before putting his thoughts to paper. Moreover, you well know what happens when one becomes involved in reflection on such central problems of the social sciences as those dealt with in your so important investigations. I can only say that it was a very great pleasure to be able, in all these months, to concern myself with your thoughts and to deliberate on them. Even where I differ with your theories I have derived immeasurable profit and stimulation from them.

It must be a misunderstanding or an error on the part of my friend Winternitz, if he told you that my work on your theory concerned the second and larger manuscript. The article which I enclose for your friendly attention is concerned, at least as it now stands, with *The Structure of Social Action*. It had originally been my plan to record my thoughts on this work in the form desired by Mr. Hayek for *Economica* and within the suggested limit of 4000 words. But it has become apparent that, at least in this first version, I am not able to deal in such brief form with the ideas contained in your work and to state the most important aspects of what I have to say about it.

Your theory deals, indeed, with the most important and central problems of all the social sciences, and such profound matters can not be reproduced in a superficial manner. Therefore, I have refrained in the course of the work from adhering to the limit set by Mr. Hayek. I have rather expressed the most important points which I have to make in a form which remains, in my opinion, concise, and with the omission of an abundance of interesting details which are dealt with in your book and which I would have liked to discuss. The result is a monstrous paper of about 20,000 words and there is probably no hope of publishing it in *Economica* in this form. I have decided, however, to work through the present version three times—it is still unfinished and it is only with some hesitation that I part with it. Yet, I imagine that even in the present form it might be welcomed above all by you, and perhaps also by one or the other critic of your work (I am thinking above all of Williams or Merton). If I do hear from you that you agree in principle with my presentation of your ideas, and if I have the opportunity to discuss this paper with you, I shall then see if I can use parts of it for an article in *Economica*. Your views on this matter will be most welcome.

As far as your manuscript on rationality is concerned, I have read it thoroughly three times and made myself a list of comments. You will see from the enclosed paper that I have tried to present your ideas with reference to this as yet unpublished manuscript of yours. The further development of your ideas to be found there has contributed a great deal to my clearer understanding of your published work. I find it, however, impossible to formulate my comments on the second and larger manuscript in writing. This shall have to wait for a personal discussion, which I am very much looking forward to.

Hence, I would like to make you the following suggestion. When your time permits, I would ask you to read and consider the enclosed article and then to grant me an opportunity for a discussion. Should your path lead you to New York and should you be able to set aside one Sunday for me —on weekdays professional demands on my time are very great—so that we can discuss at length the contents of this article and also of both your manuscripts, I would be most grateful. Otherwise, I would be most willing to come to Cambridge for a weekend, this with the main purpose of seeing and talking to you, much as I would like also to take this opportunity to greet my other friends. I would be pleased if this meeting could take place during November or in early December. At Christmas I shall not be in Chicago, as I have been invited to read a paper at the Philadelphia meeting of the American Philosophical Association. I would very much like to keep your larger manuscript until we meet, as my comments make reference to page numbers and I would like to go through them once more before our discussion, and then to have it at hand. I shall, however, inform Prof. Voegelin, who, as you may well know, has been my close friend for twenty years, that I shall send him that manuscript as soon as I no longer have need of it.

It is too bad that your group's so excellent discussions on rationality will not be taking place this semester. I was very interested to learn that you and Prof. Schumpeter are planning to publish a collection of papers. It would, of course, be delightful if this idea were to be realized and I would be very willing, if this appears desirable to you, to expand my own paper or to revise it for such a publication. Should this project not be accomplished, I would like to consider your earlier advice and submit my manuscript ["The Problem of Rationality in the Social World"—*Ed.*] to the *Journal for Social Philosophy.* I enclose with this letter a reprint of my essay, "Phenomenology and the Social Sciences," which appeared in the Husserl Memorial Volume edited by Prof. Marvin Farber [*Philosophical Essays in Memory of Edmund Husserl,* Harvard University Press, 1940—*Ed.*]. I did, of course, send you a typed copy of this essay together with the one on rationality, unfortunately without receiving any response from you. Nevertheless, I would also like you to have the printed version in your hands. Should you be interested in my paper accepted by the American Philosophical Association for its December meeting ["William James's Concept of the Stream of Thought Phenomenologically Interpreted."—Ed] I would be glad to send you a copy.

With kindest regards,

Sincerely yours,
Alfred Schutz

Parsons' Theory of Social Action:
A Critical Review by Alfred Schutz

The subtitle of Professor Parsons' important book, *The Structure of Social Action,* is "A study in Social Theory with special reference to a group of recent European writers."[1] Nevertheless, the book contains far more than this modest subtitle indicates. In fact, the abstracts of and critical remarks on the sociological theories of Marshall, Pareto, Durkheim, and Max Weber, which fill the greater part of the volume, are, in the opinion of the present writer, among the most valuable interpretations of these great masters of European sociology anywhere published on the subject. In the English language, at any rate, they are undoubtedly the best available. Most of Professor Parsons' careful and subtle analyses are certainly worth thorough discussion. Nevertheless, it is not the object of the following pages to deal with this part of Professor Parsons' work, but to reproduce and to discuss his own theory of social action, a theory which not only sums up the ideas of the above-named sociologists, but represents real progress in the evolution of the methodology of the social sciences.

A. Some Outstanding Features of Parsons' Theory [Ed.]*

As a matter of fact, Professor Parsons did not intend to write merely a secondary study. His purpose is to demon-

*Subtitles and notes added by the editor are indicated by [Ed.].

8

strate that the four men in question, though of different nationality, different social origin, different education, and different attitudes toward their science, nevertheless converge, in all essentials, upon certain fundamental postulates of the methodology and epistemology of the social sciences. These points of view, common to all the writers under consideration, are:

1. their general conception of the relationship between the theory of the social sciences and the empirical facts of social life.
2. their basic conceptual scheme of the theory of the social sciences as a theory of social action.
3. the principles of this theory of social action itself, called by Professor Parsons, "the voluntaristic theory of action."

1. EMPIRICAL FACTS IN THE SOCIAL SCIENCES AND IN EVERYDAY LIFE [ED.]

Following Professor Parsons, the views of the authors concerning the essential features of the relation between empirical social facts and social theories may be condensed as follows. Within the scientific field there are no purely empirical phenomena which are not referred to and modified by an analytical theory. The facts do not tell their own story; they must be cross-examined, analyzed, systematized, compared, and interpreted.[2] The facts science deals with and is interested in must be important for or relevant to the theoretical problem under investigation; moreover, these facts are subject to verification, and for this purpose must be formed by the logical structure of the theoretical system, which itself must be logically closed. All empirically verifiable knowledge, therefore, involves implicitly, if not explicitly, systematic theory. Not only correct observation, but also correct interpretation of the facts is the goal of scientific activity, and interpretation already presupposes reference to a theoretical scheme. Borrowing a not too fortunate definition from Professor Henderson, Professor Parsons defines a fact as an "empirically verifiable *statement* about phenomena in terms of a conceptual scheme."[3] Even if this definition could be accepted within the framework of Professor Parsons' study, it seems to me not only unusual, but rather dangerous. To be sure, Professor Parsons himself does make a clear distinction between pure phenomena and statements *about* phenomena, qualifying only the latter as "facts." Nevertheless, it is obvious that the definition advocated by Professor Parsons makes possible a confusion among three essential categories of the epistemology of sciences: *First:* facts and phenomena as they are given to the human mind. *Secondly:* interpretation of these facts and phenomena within the framework of a conceptual scheme. *Thirdly:* statements about the facts and their interpretation.

For example, the statements of physics, too, deal only with phenomena of the natural world referred to a conceptual scheme, but no physicist would agree to substitute the statements about these phenomena for the facts themselves which he observes and which are the object of his experiments. Now, the structure of a social fact is far more complicated than that of a fact in the world of physics. Whereas in the natural sciences facts can be completely described and truly classified without recourse to their "genealogy," social facts have to be *understood,* and that means they have to be interpreted as results of human activity and within the conceptual scheme of motives and goals which had led the actor to act as he did. Not only scientific theory but even everyday common sense must apply this technique of interpretation to social facts. But, if Professor Parsons' definition of facts is accepted as a starting point, it becomes rather difficult to determine the demarcation line between simple common-sense interpretation of social facts and scientific statements about social facts. I fear, therefore, that the preceding discussion concerns a principle of the structure of social facts rather than a purely terminological difference. This leads to certain consequences which will later be shown.

This critical observation does not alter my full agreement with Professor Parsons' statement that all scientific concepts of social facts already presuppose a conscious or unconscious theory of the structure of the social world, and that this theory determines the choice of problems as well as the direction of interest inherent in the selection of facts. Furthermore, I agree with Professor Parsons that, in all essentials, this point of view constitutes the common basis of the methodology of the above-named four men, regardless of differences in terminology, in where their attention is empirically focused and in their various theoretical approaches.[4]

2. THE THEORY OF THE SOCIAL SCIENCES AS A THEORY OF SOCIAL ACTION [ED.]

Thus every scientific observation of facts must be performed within a conceptual scheme which functions as a general frame of reference. For the social sciences this general frame of reference is, according to the convergent opinion of the great Western European sociologists, the theory of action.[5] This means that any phenomenon pertaining to the realm of the social sciences may be described as a system of human actions which is always capable of being broken down into ultimate "unit acts," whatever level of analysis is employed.[6]

Now, it must be stressed that the description of even the concrete components of action systems and unit acts does not comprise all the possible facts that can be known about the phenomenon in question, but only those which are relevant within the action frame of reference. To be sure, social sciences applying, concretely, the scheme of the theory of action deal also with constant data that are capable of description but not of analytic explanation within the action frame of reference.[7] As Professor Parsons says, "physical" phenomena as well as "ideas" are such data.

For instance, in dealing with a case of suicide by jumping from a bridge, the social scientist will describe it as an "act," the physical scientist as an "event." The former is interested in the motive of the actor and accepts as given that the man, if he jumps, will fall. The latter, on the other hand, is interested in the event of the fall and for him it is a given fact that the man jumps—he does not inquire why.[8] It can be stated, therefore, that the action frame of reference is not the only one in which the facts of human action can be adequately described. But, the action frame is for certain purposes, namely for the purposes of the social sciences, more adequate than the natural science scheme of space-time or any other scheme.[9]

This system of generalized social theory of action, common to the writers under consideration, is taken as a total system, a new theoretical development[10] and as being as radically different from the older utilitarian social theory as from the naive positivistic theory of action. Professor Parsons calls this theory the voluntaristic theory of action.

3. PARSONS' VOLUNTARISTIC THEORY OF ACTION [ED.]

What are its outstanding features and its elements? As we have already pointed out, all scientific conceptualization of concrete social phenomena, of concrete action systems, can always be divided into those units or parts which Parsons calls unit acts. Such unit acts involve logically the following minimum number of descriptive terms:[11]

(a) The act implies an agent, an "actor."

(b) The act must have an "end": a future state of affairs to which the process of action is oriented.

(c) The act must be initiated in a "situation" which in turn is "analyzable" into two elements: "conditions" of action over which the actor has no control, and "means" over which he has control.

(d) The act involves a certain mode of relationship between these elements, a "normative orientation" of action.

"Within the area of control of the actor," says Parsons, "the means employed cannot, in general, be conceived either as chosen at random or as dependent exclusively on the conditions of action, but must in some sense be subject to the influence of an independent, determinate selective factor, a knowledge of which is necessary to the understanding of the concrete course of action."[12] To avoid any misunderstanding it must be kept in mind that Parsons defines the term "normative" with the purpose of eliminating legal and ethical connotations: "A norm is a *verbal description* of the concrete course of action thus regarded as desirable, combined with an injunction to make certain future actions conform to this course."[13] The critical remarks made in discussing the definition of the fact as a *statement about* phenomena within a conceptual scheme may be fully applied to the definition of the norm as a *verbal description* of a course of action. Professor Parsons' tendency to substitute statements for the phenomena they deal with is certainly taken over from Pareto's theory of the role of linguistic expressions. Though from a methodological point of view Pareto's conception seems to be open to serious criticism, we shall not expand on this point. Further argumentation would not lead to greater consequences for those parts of Professor Parsons' work under consideration.

An actor, an end, a situation analyzable in turn into means and conditions, at least one selective standard in terms of which the end is related to the situation: that is the basic conceptual scheme of the unit act.[14] It has several implications. From the most important of those pointed out by Professor Parsons, we note only the following:

(a) An act is always a process in time. The time category is, therefore, basic to the scheme, and the concept of "end" already implies "attainment," "realization," "achievement," briefly a reference to a state not yet in existence, but to be brought into existence by the actor. "The end must in the mind of the actor be contemporaneous with the situation and precede the 'employment of means.' And the latter must, in turn, precede the outcome."[15] Physical time is a mode of relationship of events in space, action time a mode of relation of means and ends and other action elements.[16]

(b) There is a range of choice open to the actor with reference both to ends and means which implies the possibility of "error," of the failure to attain ends or to make the right choice of means.[17]

(c) The frame of reference of the scheme is *subjective,* that is, it deals with phenomena as they appear from the point of view of the actor. (By "objective point of view" we are to understand "from the point of view of the scientific observer of action.") The unit of reference which we are considering as the actor is not his physical organism but his "ego" or "self." The actor's body, therefore, is part of the situation of action as is the external environment. This use of the subjective point of view is more than a methodological device.[18] Certain of the fundamental elements in human behavior in society are not capable of systematic theoretical formulation without reference to subjective categories. "This is most clearly indicated by the fact that the normative elements can be conceived of as existing only in the mind of the actor."[19] "Without the subjective point of view the theory of action becomes meaningless."[20] It is the realm of applicability of the subjective point of view alone which constitutes the frame of reference called the theory of action.

The preceding features are common to every action scheme of thought. There are several possible subsystems which have been historically realized in the evolution of the social sciences since the nineteenth century. Parsons starts their description with the utilitarian system. Its outstanding features are:

1. A certain "atomism," i. e., a strong tendency to consider mainly the properties of conceptually isolated unit acts and to infer from them the properties of systems of action only by a process of "direct" generalizations.[21]

2. The means-end relationship as the normative element in the unit act, especially in the particular form called by Parsons "rational norm of efficiency." The very important term "rationality" is defined by Professor Parsons as follows: "Action is rational in so far as it pursues ends possible within the conditions of the situation, and by means which, among those available to the actor, are intrinsically best adapted to the end for reasons *understandable and verifiable by positive empirical science.*"[22]

3. Empiricism: The actor is considered to be guided by scientific or at least scientifically sound knowledge of the circumstances of his situation.

4. Randomness of ends: Utilitarian theory restricting itself to the means-end relationship, says nothing about the relations of ends to one another, nothing at least about ultimate ends.

If the active role of the actor in a utilitarian system (and, generally, in every positivistic system) is limited to the understanding of his situation and the forecasting of its future, and if in such a system ends, relative to the means-end relationship and the actor's knowledge are taken as given, then positivistic thought is caught in the "utilitarian dilemma": "Either the active agency of the actor in the choice of ends is an independent factor in action, and the end element must be random; or the objectionable implication of the randomness of ends is denied, but then their independence disappears and they are assimilated to the condition of the situation, that is to elements analyzable in terms of non-subjective categories, principally heredity and environment, in the analytical sense of biological theory."[23]

How does the "voluntaristic theory of action" overcome this dilemma? It proves the incompatibility of the action scheme with positivism and leaves room for an epistemology of a genuinely realist nature, but one involving non-empirical elements which are also non-sociological.[24]

Marshall breaks down the positivistic theory of action and the utilitarian picture of society by his refusal to accept "wants" as given data for economics and by introducing his concept of "free enterprise" which involves as a basic element certain common values, among them freedom as an end in itself and as a condition of the expression of ethical qualities.[25] Economics, as the "study of man in the everyday business of life" brings the importance of "common values" in direct connection with economic activities themselves.

Pareto overcomes the narrowness of positivistic theory by starting from the concepts of non-logical action, of residues and derivations, which lead in the interpretation of Professor Parsons to the conception of chains of intrinsic means-end relationships involving a differentiation into three sectors: ultimate ends, ultimate means and conditions, and an "intermediate sector" containing means and ends interpretable from "below" or "above."[26] This, in turn, leads to a new concept of choice: the action is oriented not only to the immediate end, but simultaneously to a plurality of different alternative ends within an integrated system of ultimate values that are either individual values or part of the "utility of the collectivity." He introduces, then, the normative or value aspect not only in concrete systems of action but in the ultimate value attitudes. Furthermore, he overcomes the individualistic "atomism" by introducing the concept of "common ends" and even of "the end, which a society should pursue."

Durkheim, though starting from a purely positivistic point of view arrives—by introducing the concepts of "non-contractual element in contract,"[27] of "anomie," of "constraint" as sanction, of the social element as consisting essentially in a common system of rules and obligations— at a "sociologism," which has eliminated its positivistic basis and is very close to the attitude of Pareto. Finally, by interpreting the symbolic form of ritual as an expression of ultimate-value attitudes, by introducing elements of action existing only in the minds of individuals, he added a whole new normative category to the structure of action.[28]

If the aforementioned three men have broken down the positivistic scheme of the theory of action in favor of the voluntaristic theory, *Max Weber* has overcome the limitations of the idealistic tradition which formed his intellectual background. The greater part of his work is devoted to the study of the social rôle of religious ideas and ultimate values. These elements, however, do not stand alone but in complex interrelation with other independent factors, such as ideas, attitudes and norms of a different kind.[29] In his methodological work Weber has demonstrated that the conception of objective scientific knowledge of any empirical subject matter is intrinsically bound up with the reality both of the normative aspect of action and of obstacles to the realization of norms, i.e., of "Wertbeziehung," which alone determines the relevant data. Furthermore, the types called "zweckrational" and "wertrational" are the theoretical equivalents of this general Weberian attitude.[30]

Summing up, the voluntaristic theory seems characterized by the introduction of an ultimate value system into the positivistic scheme. This system is integrated and not reducible to the random ends of utilitarianism. What relates the normative to the conditional elements of action is the "effort." It is necessitated by the fact that norms do not realize themselves automatically but only through action. "The basic tenet of the voluntaristic theory is that neither positively nor negatively does the methodological schema of scientifically valid knowledge exhaust the significant subjective elements of action. In so far as subjective elements fail to fit as elements of valid knowledge, the matter is not exhausted by the categories of ignorance and error, nor by the functional dependence of these elements on those capable of formulation in nonsubjective terms, nor by elements random relative to these. Positively, a voluntaristic system involves elements of a normative character."[31] They become in this system "integral with the system itself, positively interdependent with the other elements in specifically determinate ways." But "the voluntaristic system does not in the last deny an important role to conditional and other non-normative elements, but considers them as inter-dependent with the normative."[32] It is the only system which makes no restrictions on the most general formula of a system of action.

How are the unit acts technically joined in a system of action? It is not difficult to conceive of unit acts as combined to constitute more and more complex concrete systems of action. As certain degrees of complexity are reached, how-ever, an isolation of "descriptive aspects" may take place by a kind of convenient "shorthand." Parsons distinguishes two main directions of such descriptive aspects, which he calls the "relational" and the "aggregational." The first, used principally by Max Weber, consists in interpreting the acts and action systems of different individuals under the scheme of social relationships, the second in interpreting the actor as a "theoretically relevant kind of person" with particular character traits, particular attitudes and, going one step further, in describing pluralities of actors as groups.[33]

Such a system made up of unit acts in the atomistic sense would, however, only involve the possibility of unraveling the "web" of interwoven strands of the integrated system of action into concretely separable threads. That is to say, the means-end relations would be identifiable only as connect-ing a concrete act with one ultimate end through a single sequence of acts leading up to it. But the same concrete unit act is to be thought of as a means to a variety of ultimate ends, or, to use the same metaphor, "as a knot where a larger number of these threads came momentarily together only to separate again, each one to enter, as it goes on, into a variety of other knots into which only a few of those with which it was formerly combined enter with it."[34]

But the unraveling is a process of making *analytical* dis-tinctions and this leads us to a point very important for Professor Parsons' theory. He states that there are two different levels of the conceptual scheme of action—the con-crete and the analytical. First of all, he defines a *unit in a concrete system* as "the entity which constitutes the common reference of a combination of statements of fact made within a frame of reference in such a way that the combination may, for purposes of the theoretical system in question, be considered an adequate description of an entity which, within the frame of reference, conceivably exists independently." On the other hand, "an analytical element is any universal . . . of which the correspondent values . . . may be stated as facts which in part determine a class of concrete phenomena."[35]

According to these definitions on the concrete level a unit act means a concrete actual act. Thus the concrete end of a unit act means the total anticipated state of affairs so far as it is relevant to the action frame of reference. On an analytical level, however, the functional relations involved in the facts already descriptively arranged must be brought out. On this level, for example, the role of the normative-teleological elements of action must be distinguished from the role of its non-normative elements: "An end, then, in the analytical sense must be defined as the *difference* between the anticipated future state of affairs and that which it could have been predicted would ensue from the initial situation *without the agency of the actor having intervened.*"[36] Parsons writes later: "The ultimate conditions are not all those concrete features of the situation of a given concrete actor which are outside his control but are those abstracted elements of the situation which cannot be imputed to action in general. Means are not concrete tools . . . but the aspects or properties of things which actors by virtue of their knowledge of them and their control are able to alter as desired."[37]

It must be stressed that the frame of reference as developed above is common to both the concrete and the analytical level. But though it is true that in the last analysis all systems of actions are "composed" of unit acts, this does not mean that all properties of all action systems could be identified in any single unit act considered apart from its relations to others in the system. They emerge, rather, only on a certain level. So it is impossible, for instance, to say whether a single rational act is economically rational or not, without presupposing the whole system of economic action. Unit analysis, therefore, is limited by the relevance of the unit formulated to the frame of reference being employed.[38]

On the other hand, element analysis and unit analysis are not stages of scientific abstraction but two different kinds of abstraction on different levels. "Unit analysis unravels the warp of empirical reality, element analysis the woof."[39] From the perspective of element analysis, "every unit or part, concretely or conceptually isolated, constitutes a specific *combination* of the particular values of one or more analytical elements. Every 'type' is a constant set of relations of these values." The element of order in concrete phenomena consists in the fact that their values stand in certain constant modes of relation to each other. The order consists in these modes of relation plus the constancy of definition of the elements of the theoretical framework within their range of variation.

The values of analytical elements are concrete data, facts of observation or combinations of facts. Hence the action scheme as a framework of analytical elements takes on a different meaning from that which it has as a descriptive schema. Its elements have causal significance in the sense that variation in the value of any one has consequences for the values of others. Above all, the means-end schema becomes the central framework of the causal explanation of action. Furthermore, it is the specific property of this schema that it has a subjective reference. It involves a real process in the mind of the actor as well as external to it.[40] But though "it is always possible to state the facts in terms of the action frame of reference, . . . when the advance from description and unit analysis to element analysis is made, it turns out that the action categories are not analytically significant."[41]

This distinction is very important for establishing a demarcation line between historical and analytical sciences, the aim of the first being the fullest possible understanding of a class of concrete historical individuals, the aim of the latter being to develop logically coherent systems of general analytic theory. Unit or part concepts can hardly constitute the basis of independent sciences: they are adjuncts to the historical sciences. On an analytical level three great classes of theoretical systems can be distinguished: the systems of nature, action, and culture.[42]

Restricting himself to the remark that culture systems may always be considered as *products* of processes of action, but on the other hand also as conditioning elements of further action, Parsons deals only with the analytical science of action.[43] He distinguishes five analytical disciplines, each of which refers to a special subdivision of the action scheme as a frame of reference: *Economics* and the supply and demand scheme; *Political Science* and the scheme of social relations in the special form of power relationships and group schemes; *Psychology* and the personality scheme; *Technology* operating in terms of elementary means-end schemata;[44] *Sociology*—a special analytical science on the same level with economic theory as "the science which attempts to develop an analytical theory of social action systems (the term social involving a plurality of actors mutually oriented to each other's action) in so far as these systems can be understood in terms of the property of common-value integration."[45]

In this way Professor Parsons develops, starting from the theoretically well analyzed basic scheme of the unit act, the frame of reference of social theory and arrives at a well closed system of all sciences dealing with human action in general and with social phenomena in particular.

B. A Critical Examination of Parsons' Theory [Ed.]

In the preceding pages we have tried to condense some outstanding features of Professor Parsons' theory of action. Before embarking on a critical examination of several of his theses we wish to stress the many great merits of his work.

They consist, first of all, in the attempt to build up a basic methodology of the social sciences by starting from the question: what do the great masters of sociology really do in performing their concrete research work? Secondly, the attempt is made to unify their methodological remarks into a great system of theory, the theory of action, and to outline the constructive elements of such a theory as well as the implications which arise both from the historical background of the social sciences and from their logical structure.

The present writer appreciates this fundamental point of view, i.e., that the task of the social sciences cannot be considered as the mere empirical description of facts, but that all true description already necessarily presupposes a theoretical insight into the essence of human activity, to which all social phenomena refer. On the other hand, it must be regretted that Professor Parsons intentionally renounces the examination of the logical and philosophical foundations upon which a correct methodology of the social sciences must be based. It seems that an investigation of these fundamental problems of knowledge would have contributed a good deal toward greater clarity and coherence in Professor Parsons' own important and interesting theory.

All this and also the fact that the present writer can heartily agree not only with Professor Parsons' basic attitude but also with the greater part of his results should be kept in mind by the reader of the following remarks, which are not made with polemic intention but with the purpose of broadening and deepening the discussion of some of the most crucial problems of the social sciences.

There are seven topics which, in the writer's opinion, need further examination:

1. Professor Parsons' concept of concrete and analytical levels.
2. The voluntaristic theory of action and the problem of scientific knowledge on the part of the actor.

3. The problem of motives.
4. The unit act and its limits.
5. The subjective point of view.
6. Types and reality.
7. Social life and social theory.

1. CONCRETE AND ANALYTICAL LEVELS IN THE STRUCTURE OF SOCIAL ACTION [ED.]

The distinction between two different levels of the conceptual scheme of action, the concrete and the analytical, is fundamental for Parsons' theory. On the concrete level all systems of action can be broken down into unit acts with concrete actors, concrete means and concrete ends. On the analytical level, however, analysis leads to analytical elements, to "universals." Moreover, on this level the action scheme safeguarding the subjective point of view takes on a different meaning from that which it has as a descriptive schema; its elements have causal significance and it turns out in the end that the action categories are not analytically significant. On the other hand, it is stated that unit element analyses are not "stages" of scientific abstractions but two different kinds of abstraction on different levels.

It seems that Professor Parsons' distinction embraces several heterogeneous ideas, namely:

(a) *The question of different levels in scientific analyses in general and in the social sciences in particular.* What we are accustomed to call a level may be defined as the realm of an actual scientific investigation whose borders are defined by the problem under examination. The scientist, in making up his mind to study a specific topic in which he is interested, has thereby made a double decision. On the one hand, he has decided to study only *those* phenomena which are relevant to his problem and to study them only *in so far* as they are relevant to his problem. On the other hand, he has decided to accept all the other elements of his knowledge as data which remain for him "beyond question" as long as he deals with this and only this specific problem. The term "level," therefore, is another expression for the demarcation line between all that does pertain to the problem under examination and all that does not. This line is the locus of the points of actual interest to the scientist and at which he has decided to stop his further research and analysis.

But this does not mean that the decision of the scientist is arbitrary in the sense that it can disregard the intrinsic relations subsisting among all possible and, especially, among all compatible problems. On the contrary, it is possible to prove the existence of very important interdependencies among all possible systems of questions and answers and to show that there are certain key concepts the introduction of which divides the formerly homogeneous field of research into parts relevant or irrelevant to the topic under consideration. It is far beyond the purpose of this study to give even the outlines of such a system, which renews the old problem of the Aristotelian "aporetic." In this precise sense, however, Professor Parsons' distinction between element analysis and unit analysis refers undoubtedly to two different levels of research. The key concept constitutive for both of these levels will be discussed later.

(b) *The logical difference between independent parts and dependent factors.* Modern logic, and above all the studies of Edmund Husserl, have established the fundamental difference between both kinds of possible analyses.[46] One consists in breaking down wholes into parts which can exist independently of the existence of the wholes, as, if I break down, for instance, a grove into the trees which form it. This kind of analysis would correspond to Professor Parsons' unit analysis. The other consists in an abstract selection of factors which have no real existence outside the objects whose elements they are, as if I speak, for instance, of the characteristics of a certain color. Green has its hue and value, its chromatic characteristics without reference to the green objects to which this color necessarily belongs. This latter abstraction corresponds to Parsons' "element-analysis" and he is quite correct in calling these elements "universals."

But he is wrong in classifying these two possible analyses as two different levels. For element-analysis as well as unit-analysis can be performed on each level of concreteness or abstraction. Furthermore, he is wrong if he assumes, as he obviously does, that his concept of unit act does not deal exclusively with "universals." In other words, even the most "concrete" means or ends and also his concepts of "normative values" and of an "actor" are nothing but "analytical elements" in his terminology.

(c) *The subjective and the objective points of view.* Though Professor Parsons claims emphatically that the subjective point of view is the principal characteristic of element-analysis, too, it must be pointed out that, in this case, he uses the term "subjective point of view" in a quite different sense from that usually employed in his unit-analysis. In the latter a concrete actor and his concrete acts are under consideration, and its questions are: what end does the actor wish to realize; by which means; and what is his subjective knowledge about the elements of his act? Element analysis, however, is called "subjective" by Parsons only for the reason that it involves a real process within the actor's mind as well as outside of it. The shift in the meaning of the term "subjective point of view" is obvious. Further consideration will show that the lack of precision in the use of this term is in general the point in Professor Parsons' theory most open to criticism.

Is, then, Professor Parsons' distinction between concrete and analytical levels consequently ill-founded and of no value for the methodology of the social sciences? Not at all, but its real importance lies elsewhere than Professor Parsons supposes. To anticipate some later results: its real significance arises from the following dilemma. On the one hand, it is correct that social phenomena, in order to be understood, must be reduced to acts of human individuals; on the other hand, several sciences dealing with social phenomena (among them the most advanced disciplines such as economics) can and do perform their tasks without entering into analyses of individual or even collective acts. That situation is indeed bewildering and requires a thorough explanation. Parsons offers a solution, although an inconsistent one. Another attempt to overcome this dilemma will be presented later.

2. THE VOLUNTARISTIC THEORY OF ACTION AND THE PROBLEM OF SCIENTIFIC KNOWLEDGE ON THE PART OF THE ACTOR

The scheme of action which Parsons calls a "voluntaristic theory of action" should be applicable to both element analysis and unit analysis. Therefore, we may legitimately continue to examine its nature. It is regrettable that Professor Parsons nowhere indicates why he has decided to name his theory "voluntaristic." It must be assumed that his conception of normativity implies an effort on the part of the actor to accommodate his rôle as an agent to the teleological value pattern, and that this appeal to the sphere of volition has occasioned this rather strange term. The specific differences which distinguish this voluntaristic theory from the general scheme of action are obvious enough. One difference is Parsons' insight that the scheme of scientifically valid knowledge does not exhaust the subjective elements of action, and that mere reference to the categories of error and ignorance cannot be considered as a satisfactory expedient. The other difference is the introduction of elements of a normative character, that is, of elements which are integrated within the system itself.

These normative elements have a twofold function. In the first place, they have to fill in the gap not bridged by the rational (and this means for Parsons: by the scientifically verifiable) scheme of means-ends relations. To this extent the normative elements are, in Pareto's terminology, a "residual" category. Certainly, Pareto's concept of the "nonlogical elements" of action has influenced Parsons' theory to a high degree.[47]

Furthermore, the introduction of elements of a normative character eliminates the "randomness" of ends which—according to Parsons' analysis—is an outstanding feature of the utilitarian theory of action. The normative pattern creates ultimate values, integrated with and decisive for the whole structure of the system.

I agree fully with Professor Parsons that the positivistic ideal of scientifically valid knowledge is insufficient for the explanation of human acts. I would go one step further and state that it is only as an exception that the category of scientifically valid knowledge enters into the scheme of means-ends relations which the actor applies as long as he performs everyday activities. All scientific knowledge pre-supposes concepts and judgments, both of which have to be formed with an optimum of clarity, distinctness, and preci-sion. None of these qualities are typical of every day's com-mon-sense thought. Its concepts are bound to the necessities of a concrete and therefore very determined situation. They are clear only in so far as the actor's interest requires that a complex situation be elucidated. In his everyday activities the actor is not guided by the intention of finding out the real nature of facts or the real essence of causal sequences and natural laws. He is, as William James called him, "a rule-of-thumb thinker, he can deduce nothing from data with whose behavior and associates in the concrete he is unfamiliar."[48] The everyday actor has, in principle, only a partial knowledge of the world of his daily life, which he only partially understands. His propositions thus have but a very small range of applicability, namely within the con-crete situation. They are not formed with the aim of being valid for the broadest possible sector of the empirical world, a principle common to all scientific thought.

Are they therefore non-logical? Or are simple rules of experience, which merely assume the form of "recipes" by this fact alone not reasonable (or: not "rational" in the language of those who uncritically identify rationality with reasonableness)?[49] Not at all! It is *only a special form* of formal logic, of its categories and operations, which governs thought in daily life. This modified logic of daily life, the logic of "occasional judgments" as Husserl calls them, has not been developed as yet.[50] One point of departure for building this logical system would necessarily be a subjective concept of truth and verifiability and would therefore avoid the fallacies of presupposing ignorance or error on the part of the actor.

It is not our task to consider these logical problems here. But it is important for Pareto's as well as Parsons' system that the (philosophically) *naive* identification of *scientific* knowledge and *scientific* logic as such with the rational element of action is not tenable. Both authors consider the realm of non-logical or non-scientific elements as a "residual category." This tenet leads Pareto to his theory of residues and derivations as non-logical elements, and Parsons to his concept of normative values of action, which we must now discuss.

But first of all, we should show that the above conception of scientific knowledge is incompatible with the subjective point of view which Parsons correctly proclaims to be a fundamental element of the theory of action. It is true that the term "scientific" does not mean that the actor's so-called "scientific" elements of knowledge must have been verified by an empirical science. It is sufficient that the actors in the social world presume those elements to be verifiable by empirical science. But whether to be verified or merely to be verifiable: both categories are categories of the observer's knowledge, more precisely, of the knowledge of the scientist who observes acts and actors within the social world; both are therefore categories peculiar to the objective point of view. Normally, a concrete actor himself does not consider the question of whether that which his stock of common-sense experiences (his collection of recipes, his habitual convictions, his hopes and fears) represents to him as chances or risks, as likely or unlikely events, as appropriate means for given ends, are or are not verifiable by empirical science. As an actor he is not interested in the quest of certainty, but only in the chances to realize his common-sense predictions. He does not bother with the problem of whether his judgments and conclusions and their elements are true or false, provided that they are as successful in realizing his ends, as they have been successful up to the present in his own experience and in that of others.[51]

To be sure, if a situation emerges which cannot be controlled by pure routine, if the actor "stops and thinks," as Dewey says, he might refer to some empirical science, for instance, by consulting an expert as to whether the means he intends to apply are efficient enough for realizing the intended ends. But even if he does so, he does not intend to find the scientific truth but only to check his private chances for success. In the concrete performance of his action the actor cannot err. His project once realized, his action once accomplished,[52] he may very well recognize that it was a failure, that his planning was wrong, that he made a mistake in starting from presuppositions which are, for instance, incompatible with scientifically verified knowledge. The same judgment may be applied to projects and actions imagined as being realized or performed. But in looking back on an action once performed (or imagined as being performed), the so-called actor is not an actor any more. He has the same attitude to his own acts as a third observer would have. This is the detached attitude of a man who becomes disinterested in the outcome of his action, where his success or lack of it has been already tested: there is no longer a field of possibilities, open to decisions, but only accomplished events which have thus become capable of analysis and scientific criticism.

To sum up we may state our question more precisely as follows: Which of the elements pertaining to the action frame of reference are really categories in the mind of the actor and therefore subjective in the strict sense of this term; which ones are merely appropriate schemes of interpretation of the observer and, therefore, objective? Having shown the category of scientifically verifiable knowledge to be an objective one, we can go on to examine the concept of normative values. And—anticipating the result—this category, too, will reveal itself as a pure scheme of interpretation and, therefore, as incompatible with the subjective point of view.

3. NORMATIVE VALUES AND MOTIVES

The present writer must confess that, notwithstanding his most honest efforts, and despite certain explanations which Professor Parsons was kind enough to give him in private discussions, the concept of the "normative value of action" remains for him rather enigmatic. As far as I can see, Professor Parsons aims at restricting this concept to the subjective point of view. The normative value is on the one hand a pattern of action which the actor has in mind "as desirable to be realized by his own future action." To that extent it is a teleological element for the actor, or as Parsons says, a selective factor for the means under his control as well as an integrating element for the possible ends of his acts, which are no longer fixed by him at random but only within a system whose center is the ultimate-value established by the norm. On the other hand, Professor Parsons defines "norms" as verbal descriptions of a concrete course of action combined with an *injunction* to make certain future actions conform to this course. Presumably we have to interpret this latter definition in the subjective sense: the norm emerges in the mind of the actor demanding that its command be realized. But even if such an interpretation were admissible, there is obviously a great difference to be observed.

1. There is a purely *autonomous* teleological element characterized by the actor's choice and limited within his scope of freedom by certain "conditions" such as the availability of means, the chosen goal's compatibility with other goals, and so on.

2. There is a *heteronomous* command, set by the authority of some fellow-man, by law or God, by some principle of art, by social habit, custom or taste—all these being beyond the actor's control.

The *teleological element* of the normative value can indeed be conceived of as selective in the sense that—regardless of all purely "technological" factors—there is a hierarchical order, within which alone the actor considers at any given moment his ends and means (or better: his goals and means) to be integrated, to be compatible with each other. The *normative element,* however, would not be selective in the same sense. It rather limits the means and ends coming under the norm—they are no longer an object of free choice, as would be the case if the norm did not exist or were not recognized by the actor. In this sense, however, there is no norm which could not be broken down into "conditions" or "means." For each norm requires the submission of its addressee and implies some penalty for non-submission. If I am willing to accept the factual, legal, or moral sanctions which disobedience of the norm would involve in this or another world, I am free to neglect the norm. But this is exactly the situation in which the actor finds himself in a teleological dilemma. Even within the scope of free choice, each end to be realized and each means to be applied has desirable and undesirable consequences, and the actor is always faced with the choice of realizing or of abandoning his project and of accepting, with the realization or non-realization of his goal, all interfering secondary consequences which accompany it. In other words, if the concept of normative value is interpreted from a strictly subjective point of view, no reason can be discovered why the choice between means (goals) and ends ruled by a normative value should differ from any other choice that is not ruled by a normative value.

But another interpretation of Professor Parsons' theory of normative values is possible, provided we maintain a strictly subjective point of view. It must be admitted that many of his formulations suggest this second line of argument. Perhaps there is no act conceivable without a normative-value pattern. Perhaps all choice between means or ends already presupposes such a normative value without which no choice at all would be possible. Perhaps what we above called the compatibility or incompatibility of ends and means for the actor (not for the observer!) is nothing but another definition (and a worse one!) of the phenomenon that Parsons calls a "normative value." Is our whole critique merely a terminological dispute?

If this interpretation were correct we should have to ask, first of all, why the actor's knowledge of the normative pattern is presupposed by Parsons even where the actor's choice is among non-rational or non-logical acts. If, without exception, each act really presupposes the actor's knowledge of its intrinsic normative value, then there is no irrational act conceivable which would not be at least "wertrational" and therefore reasonable. Furthermore, if we must also include in the value pattern the different acts which are traditionally and especially by Max Weber called affectual and habitual acts, then we must ask what distinction exists between normative values and motives in general?

Here our critical examination of Parsons' has reached a very important topic. It is certainly strange that a theory of action designed with such accuracy and care as that of Professor Parsons should deal only superficially with the problem of motives in social action. Only in his introductory approach to the problem does he mention motives at all,[53] stating that each actor in the social world, if asked to give the meaning of his act, would enumerate certain motives. Aside from this short remark motives are referred to only once in the whole book, in his discussion of Weber's theory of "motivationally adequate understanding."[54] It must be presumed that Parsons intentionally neglected this side of the theory of action. Perhaps he considers a theory of motives to be outside the scope of a science of action and refers it to psychology. Perhaps he thinks that the theory of normative values is a more appropriate instrument for his purpose.

However, I would like to suggest that only a theory of motives can deepen the analysis of social action, provided that the subjective point of view is maintained in its strictest and unmodified sense. I have tried elsewhere[55] to outline such a theory and wish to repeat here some of its relevant features.

Excursus: A Theory of Motives Outlined in "Sinnhafter Aufbau" [Ed.]

My own starting point was to distinguish between action and behavior, the distinguishing characteristic of action being precisely that it is determined by a project which precedes it in time. Action, then, is behavior in accordance with a plan of projected behavior. Its project is neither more nor less than the action itself, conceived of and decided upon in the temporal sense of the future perfect tense. Thus the project is the primary and fundamental meaning of action.

But this is an over-simplification, which can be used only as a first approach. The meaning attributed to an experience varies according to one's whole attitude at the moment of reflection. When an action is completed, its original meaning as given in the project will be modified in the light of what action has actually been carried out. Then the completed action is open to an unlimited number of reflections which can ascribe meaning to it in the past tense. The simplest complex of meaning in terms of which an action is interpreted by the actor are the motives for the action.

But this term is equivocal and covers two different categories which have to be kept apart, the "in-order-to motives" and the "because motives." The former refer to the future and are identical with the goal or purpose for the realization of which the action itself is a means; it is a "terminus ad quem." The latter refer to the past and may be called the action's reason or cause; it is a "terminus a quo." Thus the action is determined by the project including the in-order-to motive. The project is the intended act imagined as already completed. The in-order-to motive is the future state of affairs to be realized by the projected action, and the project itself is determined by the because motive. The complexes of meaning which constitute the in-order-to motive and the because motive differ from one another in that the first is an integral part of the action itself, whereas the latter requires a special act of reflection in the pluperfect tense, which will be carried out by the actor only if there are sufficient pragmatic reasons for his doing so.

It must be added that neither the chains of in-order-to motives nor those of because motives are chosen at random by the actor performing a concrete act. On the contrary, they are organized in great subjective systems.[56] The in-order-to motives are integrated into subjective systems of planning, a life plan or plans for work and leisure, plans for "what to do the next time," timetable for today, the necessity of the hour, and so on. The because motives are grouped into systems which are appropriately treated in the American literature under the title of "social personality."[57] The self's manifold experiences of its own basic attitudes in the past, as they are condensed in the form of principles, maxims, and habits, but also of tastes, affects, etc., are the elements for building up such systems which can be personified by the actor. The latter is a very complicated problem requiring more earnest deliberation than presently possible.[58]

What are the differences between such a theory of motives and the system developed by Professor Parsons, and what is the advantage of a theory of motives? *First of all,* it can be stated that the theory of motives outlined above is strictly limited to the subjective point of view and does not contain any objective element. That is to say, exclusively subjective facts are describable from this point of view in exclusively subjective terms. Nevertheless, these subjective terms can be typified and used as a scheme of interpretation by both the partner of the actor within the social world and by the scientific observer himself.

Secondly, the intrinsic organization of both systems of motives, their organization by plans of action or by types of personality, both discard the randomness of ends assumed by the utilitarian theory of action, without entering into the metaphysical problem of ultimate values and ultimate ends. Thus the "utilitarian dilemma," as Professor Parsons calls it, has been overcome. Within the frame of reference of a theory of motives the question can never arise as to whether ultimate values do or do not exist for the actor, but only as to what is, for the actor, the degree of relevance of the different ends and in-order-to motives. The system of motives is for the actor a given one only at a certain given moment of his existence. It necessarily changes by the pure transition of inner time, from one moment to the other, if for no other reason than that in and by this transition new experiences emerge, further ones enter the foreground of interest, whereas still others fade into the background of attention, or are entirely forgotten.

This continual shift of interest, of relevance, and of attention is very complicated, but it is open to further detailed description. Perhaps this is a task for philosophy or psychology. But social theory is vitally interested in one basic fact: the system of motives (or, in Parsons' language, the system of "normative values") is above all a function of the life of the human mind *in time,* that is to say, in the "durée," to use a Bergsonian term. All really subjective description must refer to this fact, which on the other hand is hardly compatible with the conception of ultimate values or ultimate ends, or with a normativity which can only temporarily be complied with.[59]

Thirdly, the theory of motives does not state anything about the concrete substratum of the in-order-to and the because motives. These terms deal only with the form of what Professor Parsons calls the unit act, while nothing is said about the material structure of those motives. Values or norms, if they are relevant for the actor (as "Werthaltungen" or as "Normorientierungen") find their place within the scheme as well as do all non-normative elements. Furthermore, all that is subjective in the means-end relation, in the problem of rationality, of habit, of action in conformity with a pattern, etc. enters without difficulty into this scheme. And it can be shown that all the normative values Parsons has analyzed in discussing the work of the four sociologists under consideration (*Durkheim's* theory of suicide and of ritual; *Marshall's* economic categories as well as *Pareto's* residues and derivations; but certainly the whole work of *Max Weber*) are interpretable as systems of in-order-to or because motives, to the extent that the subjec-tive point of view of all these phenomena is retained.

The latter point is crucial indeed. Professor Parsons has the right insight that a theory of action would be meaning-less without the application of the subjective point of view. But he does not follow this principle to its roots. He replaces subjective events in the mind of the actor by a scheme of interpretation for such events, accessible only to the ob-server, thus confusing objective schemes for interpreting subjective phenomena with these subjective phenomena themselves. As a conscientious and extraordinarily subtle thinker, he recognizes that there must be a "certain mode of relationship" between the elements of the unit act, i.e., between the actor, the end of action and the situation itself. But he does not ask about the subjective structure of such a relationship which would have led him to study the sys-tem of motives. He fills the gap by introducing normative values, which give indeed a very helpful scheme for inter-preting the motives of social action and are applied with the greatest success by many renowned sociologists.

But regardless of several statements, quoted above, that normative value interpretation is not only compatible, but even in a certain degree correlative with the subjective point of view, the only question Professor Parsons never asks is, what really does happen in the mind of the actor from his subjective point of view. His analyses only answer the question of how a theoretical scheme can be established which is capable of explaining what may happen or what may be considered as happening in the mind of the actor. And so Parsons is not concerned with finding out the truly subjective categories, but seeks only objective categories for the interpretation of subjective points of view.

But is Professor Parsons not right in doing so? It must be admitted that this problem of dealing with subjective phe-nomena in objective terms is *the* problem for the methodol-ogy of the social sciences. The reader might already impatiently ask why the subjective point of view is defended here with such stubbornness. Apparently, it does not seem to lead to a system which is of practical use to social scientists, but which obviously ends in an impasse of solipsism and psychologistic subtitles, both outside the scope of social science. We must ask him for a little more patience. The theory of social action—this important feature of modern sociology, in the establishing of which Parsons' share of merit cannot be overestimated—stands or falls with the results of an analysis of the relation between the subjective point of view and the terms which sociologists actually use in performing their concrete research work. But before embarking on these analyses we have to discuss one further point in Professor Parsons' theory which seems to us intermingled with the principle of subjectivity.

4. THE LIMITS OF THE UNIT ACT

Professor Parsons defines "unit acts" as the last elements into which a concrete system of action can be broken down.[60] There are four characteristics of a unit act: a given actor, a given end, a given situation (including conditions and means of the act), and a given normative value orientation as the relationship between those other elements. Up to now, we have examined only the interrelation between the normative value orientation and the subjective point of view. The conclusion was that the methodological function of the normative value, subjectively interpreted, does not differ from that of other in-order-to and because motives and that only from an objective point of view might some motives conform to Professor Parsons' concept of "values with normative character." We will now try to show that all the other features of the unit act enumerated by Professor Parsons undergo a shift in their intrinsic meaning, if they are interpreted either from the subjective or from the objective point of view.

Let us start with the principal question. Is it logically possible to break down an action system into unit acts as its last available elements? We wish to defend the thesis that this "breaking down" will and must lead to radically different results according to whether it is performed by the actor or by the observer. This difference is not accidental; it is essentially determined by the logical structure peculiar to the understanding of the alter ego. The very terms "system of actions" and even "action" itself are equivocal in so far as they require a subscript, indicating for *whom* the concrete occurrence under consideration presents itself as an "action" or as a "system of actions."

The deeper reason for this essential determination lies in the specific attitude of the actor toward his own act. Naively conducting his everyday affairs, the actor finds himself right from the beginning directed by several subjective systems which organize his own life. These are systems of planning and projecting, of goals to be attained, of happiness to be realized, of duties to be performed, of evils to be warded off. They determine the scope of all the actor's possible activities, as well as the procedure for each of his concrete acts, even the humblest ones. Further analysis shows that these systems or organization are systems of subjectively consistent in-order-to motives, as we have just called them, which are framed within more or less conscious "life-plans." These systems again are based on systems of subjectively consistent because motives, such as principles, maxims, etc.

A very important question is certainly: how may such systems emerge within the stream of an individual's life and how do they become organized? This question pertains to the great problem of relevance and it is above all the task of a scientific study of personality to further its examination.[61]

But we need not begin to examine it here. We may restrict ourselves to the assumption that such consistent plans are given for each actor. Within the hierarchical order of those consistent motives, called plans and maxims of subjective life, each project of action occupies a well determined position.

Therefore, it is the systems of motives alone, which the actor has built up so far and which he still accepts as consistent principles for organizing his life, which determine for him the meaning of the concrete act he is going to perform. This fundamental thesis does not contradict the fact that, apparently, a great deal of our everyday activities are performed without the presence of clearly understood and well circumscribed projects in the mind of the actor. But that only means either that such projects do not immediately precede the act and are hidden in the past of the actor's inner life, or that they are temporarily out of view and, if we may say so, hidden in the future.

As an illustration of *the first case,* consider routine-work, action ruled by habits, skills or recipes; these are projected actions, too, though the project does not *immediately* precede the performance of the concrete act. But there did once exist a series of projected and deliberated acts carried out in order to form the habit, acquire the skill, find out the recipe. Their basic motive was the actor's insight that he finds himself faced with certain ends which may be called "constant" ends because they have to be realized again and again within the framework of consistent plans.

As an example of *the second case* we have only to remember that projects of action embracing a long period of time are divided by the natural rhythm of life into sub-periods defined by intermediate ends. For instance, the man who wants to write a book cannot perform this work at a stroke. He has to divide his project into partial tasks, the ends of which, however, depend on one steadily maintained basic aim. The paragraph he has to put down today or the sentence he is just working out are planned in order to finish the projected book, which itself, perhaps, forms only a part of the author's thought.

Taking all this into account, we may state that, for the actor, nothing other than the span of his project constitutes the unit of his act. In this statement the term "project" also includes the horizon of the actor's consistent life plans, in so far as the concrete, future state of affairs to be realized by the projected action has its more or less well-defined position within these plans. It is for several reasons that we intentionally call it "more or less well-defined." *First of all,* the whole system of life-plans, although within itself consistent at every moment, necessarily changes with the transition of the actor's self from one moment of his inner life to the next. As we said before, it is the system of life-plans which determines the full meaning of the concrete act for the actor. Therefore, this meaning itself changes with the continuous modification of the whole system. *Secondly,* the system of life-plans is only partially known to the actor in its fully explicit form and is only partially caught by the ray of actual attention and thereby rendered relevant. In any given moment, there is a brightly illuminated nucleus surrounded by a horizon of growing darkness. Together they constitute the explicable, though not explicated background against which the projected concrete act stands out. And, as I would like to repeat, it is the span of the project, thus determined, which for its part creates the unity of the act.

But all this is open only to the knowledge of the actor himself and remains beyond the observer's control and even beyond his approach. For, the observer has no other access to the action of the actor but the acts once accomplished. What the observer can observe are only segments of the actor's performed activity. If he would really and honestly begin to describe what happens in the actor's mind in performing an action, however humble and insignificant, he would have to enter into the whole process of the actor's stream of thought, with the whole history of his personality, with all his subjective life-plans and their genesis, with all his skill and experiences, and with all his expectations concerning future states of affairs. To be able to do so, the observer would have had to run through all the stages of the inner life of the person observed, and that in the same succession and at the same pace, and experiencing it in the same fullness as did the person observed. And that means the observer would have to be identical with the one observed—an insight which Bergson already attained in his first book.[62]

Having this problem clearly in view, we must seriously

ask, "When does an act start and when is it accomplished?" In truth, no one else is qualified to answer this question but the actor himself. He alone knows the span of his plans and projects. He alone knows their horizons and, therefore, the elements constituting the unity of his acts. He alone, therefore, is qualified to "break down" his own action system into genuine "unit acts." The observer, on the contrary, decides at his discretion whether the observed action must be interpreted as accomplished or as part of a greater work in progress. For him the unity of the act, its beginning and its end, is, then, no longer identical with the span of the actor's project but is defined by that segment of the actor's activity which the observer has selected as object of his consideration. In this manner the term "unit act," which has its native place within the sphere of subjectivity, assumes quite a different meaning if it is interpreted from the objective point of view. But by no means can we speak of the unit act from the subjective point of view and accept at the same time the supposition that the limits of this unit are constituted or drawn by the observer.

Consequently, all the features characterizing the unit act according to Professor Parsons' description are genuinely subjective terms, interpretable and understandable above all from the subjective point of view, and suffering a shift in meaning when transposed into the realm of objectivity. Concerning the term "end" this thesis is, we suppose, self-explanatory. Only the actor knows the real end, or better, the real goal of his action. The observer can never decide whether what he considers to be an end is such for the actor, too, or only an intermediate end, a means, therefore, for the realization of the ultimate goal included within the span of the actor's project. On the contrary, for the observer the term "end" indicates the state of affairs as obviously brought about by the actor's already accomplished act.

Furthermore, it is easy to understand that the term "situation" refers, from the subjective point of view, to the already projected end, which alone defines the elements relevant for its attainment. As far as the distinction between the two components of the situation ("means" and "conditions") is concerned, the question as to whether the actor does or does not have control over them refers to his stock of knowledge and experience at the time of his projecting the act. So interpreted, the demarcation line between the two factors of "situation," namely between ends and conditions of the act, can be drawn only by the actor himself, and from an objective (i.e., from a "scientific") point of view it may happen that what the actor considers as means pertain really to the conditions of the concrete act, and vice versa. For, from the objective point of view, conditions are those elements of the situation over which, according to the verifiable empirical knowledge of others, the actor could not have had any control, whether or not the actor had any real knowledge of his inability to control them or to appreciate their relevance.

It is a little more difficult to show that also the term "actor" can be interpreted from a subjective as well as from an objective point of view. Professor Parsons is quite right in pointing out that the concept "actor" is an abstraction. But this does not allow one to conclude that the "actor" has to be contrasted with the "biological individual," with the "living organism." These terms, too, are "abstractions" from the basic conception of the "individual human being," which is neither more nor less "actor" or "biological individual" than it is a "creature" from the theological point of view or a "physical person" from the legal. The functional meaning of all these abstractions, as far as they are made in the sciences, is the exact circumscription of that aspect of human personality which thus alone becomes relevant for the basic problems of the respective science.

The observer in everyday life performs other abstractions from the subjective point of view. For instance, such abstractions are made by the partner of the "actor" in the social life-world, a problem to be returned to later. Here we are interested in the fact that there are subjective correlates to those abstractions which have been built up by the scientist or by the actor's observer in everyday life. The problem we have in mind is one of the most important in the theory of personality; it is the problem of the "roles" the ego assumes within the social world.

Applied to our problem of action we can say that the ego (which afterwards will be called the "actor") decides, while planning its act, which factors of its personality are to operate, or, to use a term from William James, which of his several "selves" is to partake in the action. This "role" does not and cannot coincide with the concept of "actor" formed by the observer. The latter concept characterizes a typified social person, that part of the alter ego under observation which expresses itself in the performed act interpreted as a typical one. The former concept, however, the role assumed by the ego, is a token of the personality as far as its structurization appears to the ego itself. Only he who, in retrospect, will be called an actor can decide on and describe the role he is going to assume by performing his projected act, its location in a more or less central stratum of his personality, its character of greater or lesser intimacy, etc. As will be shown below, the distinction between the subjective and the objective concept of "actor" is of the greatest importance for the theory of ideal-types.[63]

Summing up: We have shown that the concept "unit act" as well as each of its outstanding features enumerated by Professor Parsons might be interpreted from either a subjective or an objective point of view, but that in each case the meaning of these terms is different. Professor Parsons claims, as noted above, that the subjective point of view is the only acceptable one for any theory of social action, and the present writer cannot sufficiently emphasize the importance of this insight. Nevertheless, as I mentioned before, Professor Parsons does not really analyze the subjective categories of action, but rather the objective categories for scientifically describing the actor's subjective points of view.

This attempt seems to need further examination, since Professor Parsons abstains from showing, on the one hand, why reference to the subjective point of view is an indispensable prerequisite for the theory of action and, on the other hand, how it is possible to deal with subjective phenomena in terms of an objective conceptual scheme. We shall start with the study of the first question and hope to show that the subjective point of view is not only *a possible means* of describing the social world, but even *the only one* adequate to the reality of social phenomena—as conceived under the scheme of reference of social action.

5. THE SUBJECTIVE POINT OF VIEW IN THE SOCIAL SCIENCES[64]

At first sight it is not easy to understand why the subjective point of view should be preferred in the social sciences. Why always address ourselves to this mysterious and not too interesting tyrant of the social sciences called the subjectivity of the actor? Why not honestly describe in honestly objective terms what really happens, and that means speaking our own language, the language of qualified and scientifically trained observers of the social world? And if it be objected that these terms are but artificial conventions created by our "will and pleasure," and that, therefore, we cannot utilize them for real insight into the meaning which social acts have for those who act, but only for our interpretation, we could then answer that it is precisely this building up of a system of conventions and an honest description of the world which *is* and is alone the task of scientific thought; that we scientists are no less sovereign in our system of interpretation than the actor is free in setting up his system of goals and plans; that we social scientists in particular have but to follow the pattern of the natural sciences, which have performed, with the very methods we should abandon, the most wonderful work of all time; and, finally, that it is the essence of science to be objective, valid not only for me, or for me and you and a few others, but for everyone, and that scientific propositions do not refer to my private world but to the one and unitary life-world common to us all.

The last part of this thesis is incontestably true. But there is no doubt that even a fundamental point of view can be imagined, according to which the social sciences have to follow the pattern of the natural sciences and to adopt their methods. Pushed to its logical conclusion it leads to the method of behaviorism. To criticize this principle is beyond the scope of the present study. We restrict ourselves to the remark that radical behaviorism stands and falls with the basic assumption that there is no possibility of proving the intelligence of one's "fellow-man." It is highly probable that he is an intelligent human being, but this is a "weak fact" not capable of verification.[65]

Yet, it is not then easy to understand why an intelligent individual should write books for others or even meet others at congresses where it is reciprocally proven that the intelligence of the Other is a questionable fact. It is even less understandable why the same authors who agree that there is no verifying the intelligence of other human beings have such confidence in the principle of verifiability itself, which can be realized only through cooperation with others by mutual control. Furthermore, they do not feel inhibited about starting their deliberations with the dogmatic assertions that language exists, that speech reactions and verbal reports are legitimate methods of behavioristic psychology,[66] that propositions in a given language are meaningful, without considering that language, speech, verbal report, proposition, and meaning already presuppose intelligent alter egos, capable of understanding the language, of interpreting the proposition, and of verifying the meaning. But the phenomena of understanding and of interpreting cannot themselves be explained as pure behavior, provided we do not resort to the subterfuge of a "covert behavior" which evades description in behavioristic terms.[67]

These few critical remarks, however, do not touch upon the center of our problem. Behaviorism as well as every other objective scheme of reference in the social sciences has, of course, as its chief purpose the explanation using scientifically correct methods of what really happens in the social world of our everyday life. It is, of course, neither the goal nor the purpose of any scientific theory to design and to describe a fictitious world having no reference whatsoever to our common-sense experience and being therefore without any practical interest to us. The founders of behaviorism had no other purpose than that of describing and explaining real human acts within a real human world. But the fallacy of their theory consists in the substitution of a fictional world for social reality by the promulgation of methodological principles represented as being appropriate to the social sciences which, though proved successful in other fields, prove a failure in the realm of intersubjectivity.[68]

But behaviorism is only one form of objectivism in the social sciences, though the most radical one. The student of the social world does not find himself placed before the inexorable alternative either of accepting the strictest subjective point of view, and, therefore, of studying the motives and thoughts in the mind of the actor, or of restricting himself to the description of the overt behavior and of admitting the behaviorist's tenet of the inaccessibility of the Other's mind and even the unverifiability of the Other's intelligence. Rather, it is possible to conceive of a basic attitude—adopted, in fact, by several of the most successful social scientists—which accepts naively the social world with all the alter egos and institutions in it as a meaningful universe, i.e., meaningful for the observer whose only scientific task consists in describing and explaining his and his co-observers' experiences of it.

To be sure, these scientists admit that phenomena such as nation, government, market, price, religion, art, or science refer to activities of other intelligent human beings and constitute for them the world of their social life; they admit furthermore that alter egos have created this world by their activities and that they orient their further activities to its existence. Nevertheless, so they pretend, we are not obliged to go back to the subjective activities of those alter egos and to their correlates in their minds in order to give a description and explanation of the facts of this social world. Social scientists, they contend, may and should restrict themselves to describing what this world means to them, neglecting what it means to the actors within this social world. Let us collect the facts of this social world, as our scientific experience may present them, in a reliable form; let us describe and analyze these facts; let us group them under pertinent categories and study the regularities in their shape and development which then emerge, and we shall arrive at a system of the social sciences, discovering the basic principles and the analytical laws of the social world. Having once reached this point the social sciences may confidently leave the subjective analyses to psychologists, philosophers, metaphysicians, or whatever else you like to call the idle people who concern themselves with such problems. And the defender of such a position may ask whether it is not this scientific ideal which the most advanced social sciences are about to realize. Look at modern economics! The great progress made in this field dates exactly from the decision of some advanced minds to study curves of demand and supply and to discuss equations of prices and costs instead of striving hard and in vain to penetrate the mystery of subjective wants and subjective values.

Such a position is, without doubt, not only possible but is even accepted by the majority of social scientists. Doubtless, too, on a certain level real scientific work may be performed and has been performed without entering into the problem of subjectivity. We can go far ahead in the study of social phenomena, such as social institutions of all kinds, social relations, and even social groups, without at all leaving the basic frame of reference, which can be formulated as follows: what does all this mean for us, the scientific observers? We can develop and apply a refined system of abstraction for this purpose which intentionally eliminates the actor in the social world, with all his subjective points of view, and we can even do so without coming into conflict with the experiences derived from social reality. Masters in this technique—and there are many in all fields of social research—will always guard against leaving the consistent level within which this technique may be adopted and will therefore adequately confine their problems.

All this does not alter the fact that this type of social science does not deal directly and immediately with the world of everyday life, common to us all, but with skillfully and expediently chosen idealizations and formalizations of the social world which are not repugnant to its facts. Nor does this type of science make the less indispensable reference to the subjective point of view on other levels of abstraction, if the original problem under consideration is modified. But then—and that is an important point—this reference to the subjective point of view *can* always be made and should be made. As this social world remains, under any aspect whatsoever, a very complicated cosmos of human activities, we can always go back to that "forgotten man" of the social sciences, to the actor in the social world whose doing and feeling lie at the bottom of the whole system. We, then, try to understand him in his doings and feelings and to grasp the state of mind which induced him to adopt specific attitudes towards his social environment.

In this case, the answering of our question, "What does this social world mean for me, the observer?", has as a prerequisite the answering of the quite different questions, "What does this social world mean for the observed actor within this world, and what did he mean by his acting within it?" With these questions we no longer naively accept the social world and its current idealizations and formalizations as ready-made and meaningful beyond all doubt, but undertake to study the process of idealizing and formalizing as such, the genesis of the meaning which social phenomena have for us as well as for the actors, the mechanism of the activity by which human beings understand one another and themselves. We are always free, and sometimes obliged, to do so.

6. TYPES AND REALITY [ED.]

The possibility of studying the social world from different points of view reveals the fundamental importance of the approach of Professor Znaninecki quoted above. Each social phenomenon may be studied under the scheme of reference of social relations or of social groups (we may be allowed to add the scheme of social institutions), but our study could take place with equal legitimacy under the scheme of social acts or of social persons. The first group of schemes of reference is the objective one; such schemes will do good service if applied exclusively to problems belonging to the sphere of objective phenomena for whose explanation their specific idealizations and formalizations have been designed, provided, however, that they do not contain any inconsistent element or elements incompatible with the other (the subjective) schemes and with our common-sense experience of the social world in general. Mutatis mutandis the same thesis is valid for all subjective schemes.[69]

In other words, the scientific observer decides to study the social world within an objective or a subjective frame of reference. This decision delimits from the beginning that section of the social world (or, at least, the aspect of such a section) which becomes capable of being studied once that scheme has been chosen. The basic postulate of the methodology of social science, therefore, must be the following: choose a scheme of reference adequate to the problem you are interested in, consider its limits and possibilities, make its terms compatible and consistent with one another, and having once accepted it, stick to it![70] If, on the other hand, the ramifications of your problem lead you while your work progresses to accept other schemes of reference and interpretation, do not forget that with the change of scheme all terms formerly used necessarily undergo a shift in meaning. To preserve the consistency of your thought you have to see to it that the "subscript" of all the terms and concepts you use is the same!

This is the real meaning of the so often misunderstood postulate of "purity of method." It is harder than it seems to comply with it. Most fallacies in the social sciences can be reduced to a mergence of subjective and objective points of view which, unnoticed by the scientists, arose while transgressing from one level to the other in the progress of the scientific work. These are the dangers of mixing up subjective and objective points of view in the concrete work of the social scientist. But a theory of social action must retain the subjective point of view to its fullest degree, if such a theory is not to lose its basic foundations, namely its reference to the social world of everyday life and experience. Safeguarding the subjective point of view is the only, but a sufficient, guarantee that social reality will not be replaced by a fictional non-existing world constructed by some scientific observer.

To clarify this matter further let us forget for a moment that we are social scientists observing the social world with a detached and disinterested mind. Let us see how each of us interprets the social world common to us all, in which he lives and acts just as any man among his fellow-men, a world which he conceives of as a field of his possible actions and orientations, organized around his person under the specific scheme of his plans and the relevances deriving from them, but mindful, too, that the same social world is the field of other peoples' possible action and from their point of view organized around them in an analogous manner.

This world is always given to me from the start as an organized one. I was, so to speak, born into this organized social world and I grew up in it. Through learning and education, through experiences and experiments of all kinds, I acquire a certain ill-defined knowledge of this world and its institutions. Above all I am interested in the objects of this world in so far as they determine my own orientation, as they further or hinder the realization of my own plans, as they constitute an element of my situation, which I have to accept or to modify, as they are the source of my happiness or discontent—in a word, in so far as they *mean* anything to me. This meaning for me implies that I am not satisfied with the pure knowledge of the existence of such objects; I have to understand them, and this means I have to be able to interpret them as possible relevant elements for possible acts or reactions I might perform within the scope of my life plans.

But from the beginning this orientation through understanding occurs in cooperation with other human beings: this world has meaning not only for me but also for you and you and for everyone else. My experience of the world justifies and corrects itself through the experience of Others with whom I am interrelated by common knowledge, common work, and common suffering. The world, interpreted as the possible field of action for all of us, this is the first and most primitive principle of organization of my knowledge of the external world in general. Afterwards, I discriminate between *natural things,* which may be defined as things essentially given, such as they are, to me and to you and to everyone else independent of any human act or interference, and, on the other hand, *social things,* which are understandable only as products of human activity, my own activity or that of others.[71]

Concerning *natural things* my "understanding" is limited to the insight into their existence, variation and development, in so far as these elements are compatible, first of all, with my other experiences and the experiences of Others within the natural world in general and, secondly, with the basic assumptions concerning the structure of this world which we all accept by common consent. Within these limits prediction (though only of likelihood) is possible for us all. In my opinion and in the opinion of us all, this thing here is a wild apple-tree. This implies that it will bear blossoms in spring, leaves in summer, fruit in fall, and become bare in winter. If we want to have a better view, we may climb to its top. If we need relaxation in summer, we may rest in its shade. If we are hungry in fall, we may taste its fruits. All these possibilities are independent of any human agency; the cycle of natural events revolves without our interference.[72]

If you wish to do so there is no objection to calling this organized knowledge of natural facts an "understanding" of them. But used in this larger sense the term "understanding" means nothing other than the reducibility of known and tested facts to other known and tested facts. If I consult an expert in the physiology of plants in order to learn what is really behind the aforenamed cycle in vegetative life, he will refer me to the chemistry of chlorophyl or to the morphological structure of cells. In short, he will "explain" the facts by reducing them to others, which have a greater generality and which have been tested in a broader field.

Quite another "understanding" is peculiar to *social things,* (this term embracing also human acts). In this case it is not sufficient to refer the fact under consideration to other facts or things. I cannot understand a social thing without reducing it to the human activity which has created it and, going beyond, without referring this human activity to the motives out of which it sprang. I do not understand a tool without knowing the purpose for which it was designed, a sign or a symbol, without knowing what it stands for, an institution, if I am unfamiliar with its goals, a work of art if I neglect the intentions of the artist which it realizes.

Above all, I cannot understand other people's acts without knowing the in-order-to or the because motives of such acts. To be sure, there are manifold degrees of understanding. I do not need to (even more, I cannot) grasp the full ramifications of other people's motives, with their horizons of individual life plans, their background of individual experiences, their references to the unique situations by which they are determined. As said before, such an ideal understanding would presuppose full identity of my stream of thought with that of the alter ego, and that would mean an identity of both our selves. It suffices, therefore, that I can reduce the Other's act to its typical motives, including their reference to typical situations, typical ends, typical means, etc.

On the other hand, there are also different degrees of my knowledge of the actor himself, degrees of intimacy and anonymity. I may reduce the product of human activity to the agency of an alter ego with whom I share present time and present space, but then this other individual may be an intimate friend of mine or a passenger whom I meet for the first time and will most likely never meet again. It is not even necessary that I should have met the actor personally in order to have an approach to his motives. I can, for instance, understand the acts of a foreign statesman and discuss his motives without ever having met him or even without having seen a picture of him. The same is true for individuals who have lived long before my own time. I can understand the acts and motives of Caesar as well as of the caveman who left no other testimony of his existence than the flint hatchet exhibited in the showcase of some museum.

But it is not even necessary to reduce human acts to a more or less well-known individual actor. To understand them it is sufficient to find typical motives of typical actors which explain the act as a typical one arising out of a typical situation. There is a certain conformity in the acts and motives of priests, soldiers, servants, farmers everywhere and at every time. Moreover, there are acts of such a general type that it is sufficient to reduce them to "somebody's" typical motives in order to make them understandable.

All this must be carefully investigated as an essential part of the theory of social action. [73] Summing up, we come to the conclusion that social things are understandable only if they can be reduced to human activities; and human activities can be made understandable only by showing their in-order-to or because motives. This fact has its deeper reason in that I am able to understand other people's acts while living naively in the social world only if I can imagine that I myself would perform analogous acts if I were in the same situation as the Other, directed by the same because motives or oriented by the same in-order-to motives—all these terms understood in the restricted sense of a "typical" analogy, a "typical" sameness, as explained above.

That this assertion is true can be demonstrated by an analysis of the social action in the more precise sense of this term, namely, of an action which involves the attitudes and actions of Others and is oriented to them in its ongoing course.[74] Up to now, this study has dealt only with action as such without analyzing the modifications which occur within the general scheme with the introduction of certain social elements proper, such as mutual correlation and intersubjective adjustment. That is to say, we have observed the attitude of an isolated actor without making any distinction as to whether this actor is occupied with handling a tool or acting with others and for others, motivated by others and motivating them.[75]

The analysis of this topic is very complicated and we have to restrict ourselves to sketching its outlines. All social relations as they are understood by me, a human being living naively in a social world centered around him, can be shown to have their prototype in the social relation between myself and an individual alter ego with whom I am sharing space and time. My social act, then, is oriented not only to the physical existence of this alter ego but also to the Other's act which I expect to initiate by my own action. I can, therefore, say that the Other's reaction is the in-order-to motive of my own act. The prototype of all social relationship is an intersubjective concatenation of motives. If in projecting my act I imagine that you will understand my action and that this understanding will induce you to react, on your part, in a certain way, then I anticipate that the in-order-to motives of my own acting will become because motives of your reaction, and vice-versa.

Let us take a very simple example: I ask you a question. The in-order-to motive of my act is not only the expectation that you will understand my question, but also to get your answer. More precisely, I reckon *that* you will answer, leaving undecided what the content of your answer may be. *Modo futuri exacti* I anticipate in projecting my own act that you will have answered my question in some way or other. This means I think there is a fair chance that the understanding of my question will become a because motive for the answer, which I expect you to give. The question, we may say, is the because motive of the answer, while the answer is the in-order-to motive of the question. This inter-relationsship between my own and your motives is a well-tested experience of mine, though, perhaps, I have never had any explicit knowledge of its complicated inner mechanism. But I had on innummerable occasions felt myself induced to react to another's act (which I had interpreted as a question addressed to me) with a kind of behavior whose in-order-to motive was my expectation that the Other, the questioner, might interpret my behavior as an answer. Over against this experience I know that I have succeeded frequently in provoking another person's answer by my own act of questioning, and so on. Therefore, I feel I have a fair chance of getting your answer when I shall have once realized that action of questioning.

This short and incomplete analysis of a rather trivial example shows the great complications inherent in the problem of the social act, but it also gives an idea of the dimensions of the field to be explored by a theory of action that is worthy of its name. We do not intend to enter further into this topic here, but some conclusions should be drawn from our example concerning the subjective point of view and its role for the actor in the social world.

The social world in which I live as one connected with others through manifold relations is for me an object to be interpreted as meaningful. It makes sense to me, but by the same token I am sure it makes sense to Others too. I suppose, furthermore, that my acts, oriented to Others, will be understood by them in a way analogous to the way I understand the acts of Others oriented to me. More or less naively I presuppose the existence of a common scheme of reference for both, for my own acts and the acts of Others. I am interested above all not in the overt behavior of Others, not in their performance of gestures and bodily movements, but in their intentions, and this means I am interested in the in-order-to motives for the sake of which Others act as they do, and in the because motives based on which they act as they do.

Convinced that Others want to express something by their act or that their act has a specific position within a common frame of reference, I try to catch the meaning which the act in question has, particularly for my co-actors in the social world, and, until presented with counter-evidence, I presume that this meaning for them, the actors, corresponds to the meaning their act has for me. As I have to orient my own social acts to the because motives of Others' social acts oriented to me, I must always find out their in-order-to motives and disentangle the web of social interrelationship by interpreting other people's acts from the subjective point of view of the actor. That is the great difference between the attitude of a man who lives amidst manifold social relations in which he is interested as a participant and the pure observer who is disinterested in the outcome of a social situation in which he does not participate and which he studies with a detached mind.

There is a further reason why man living naively among others in the social world tries above all to find out the motives of his co-actors. Motives are never isolated elements but grouped in great and consistent systems of hierarchical order. Having grasped a sufficient number of elements of such a system, I have a fair chance of completing the "empty" positions of the system by correct conjectures. Basing my assumption on the inner logical structure of such system of motives, I am able to make inferences concerning those parts which remain hidden with a considerable likelihood of proving them correct. But, of course, all this presupposes interpretation from the subjective point of view, i.e., answering the question, "What does all this mean for the actor?"

This practical attitude is adopted by us all in so far as we do not merely observe a social situation which does not touch us, but act and react within the social world. This is precisely the reason why the subjective point of view must be accepted by the social sciences too. Only this methodological principle gives us the necessary guarantee that we are dealing in fact with the real social life-world common to us all, which, even as an object of theoretical research, remains a system of reciprocal social relations. All these relations are built up by mutual subjective interpretations of the actors within the social world.

7. SOCIAL LIFE AND SOCIAL THEORY

But if the principle of safeguarding the subjective point of view in the social sciences were even admitted, how is it possible to deal scientifically—and that means in objective, conceptual terms—with such subjective phenomena? The greatest difficulty lies, first of all, in the specific attitude the scientific observer has adopted towards the social world. As a scientist—not as a man among other men, which he is, too —he is not a participant in social interrelationsship. He does not participate in the living stream of mutual testing of the in-order-to motives of his own acts by the reactions of others, and vice versa. Strictly speaking, as a pure observer of the social world the social scientist does not act. In so far as he "acts scientifically" (publishing papers, discussing problems with others, teaching) his activity is performed *within* the social world: he acts as man among other men, dealing with science, but he no longer has, then, the specific attitude of a scientific observer. This attitude is character- ized by the fact that it is performed in complete aloofness. To become a social scientist the observer must make up his mind to step out of the social world, to drop any practical interest in it, and to restrict his in-order-to motives to the honest description and explanation of the social world which he observes.

But how should this task be performed? Not being able to communicate directly with the actors within the social world, he is unable to verify directly the data he has ob- tained about the actors from the different sources of infor- mation open to him within the social world. To be sure, he himself has, as a man among others, immediate experiences of the social world. In that capacity he can send out ques- tionnaires, hear witnesses, establish test-cases. From these and other sources he gathers data which he will later use, once he retires to the solitude of the theoretician. But his theoretical task as such begins with the building up of a conceptual scheme under which his information about the social world may be grouped.

It is one of the outstanding features of modern social science to have described the device social scientists use in building up their conceptual scheme. It is the great merit of the four social scientists analyzed by Professor Parsons in his "Structure of Social Action," and above all of Max Weber, to have developed this technique in all its fullness and clarity. This technique consists in replacing the human beings, which the social scientist observes as an actor on the social stage, by puppets which he creates, in other words, in constructing ideal types of actors. This is done in the following way.[76]

The scientist observes certain events within the social world as caused by human activity and he begins to establish a type of such events. Afterwards these typical acts are coordinated with typical because motives and in-order-to motives which he assumes to be invariable within the mind of an imaginary actor. Thus he constructs a personal ideal type, which means a model of an actor whom he imagines to be gifted with consciousness. But it is a consciousness restricted in its content to only those elements necessary for the performance of the typical acts under consideration. It contains all these elements completely but nothing beyond them. He imputes to it constant in-order-to motives corresponding to the goals which are realized within the social world by the acts under consideration; furthermore, he ascribes to it constant because motives of such a structure that they may serve as a basis for the system of presupposed constant in-order-to motives; finally, he bestows on this ideal type such segments of life plans and such stocks of experiences as are necessary for the imaginary horizons and backgrounds of the puppet actor. The social scientist places these constructed types in a setting which contains all the elements of the real life situation relevant for the performance of the typical act under consideration. Moreover, he associates with this first ideal type other personal ideal types having motives that are apt to provoke typical reactions to the first and his typical acts.

Thus the social scientist arrives at a model of the social world or, better, at a reconstruction of it. It contains all relevant elements of the social event chosen as a typical one by the scientist for further examination. It is a model which complies perfectly with the postulate of the subjective point of view. For from the outset the puppet type is imagined as having the same specific knowledge of the situation—including means and conditions—which a real actor would have in the real social world. From the outset the subjective motives of a real actor performing a typical act are implanted as constant elements of the specious consciousness of the personal ideal type. It is the purpose of the personal ideal type to play the role an actor in the social world would have to adopt in order to perform the typical act. Since the type is constructed in such a way that it performs exclusively typical acts, the objective and subjective elements in the formation of unit acts coincide.

On the other hand, the formation of the type, the choice of the typical event, and the elements considered as typical are all conceptual constructions which can be discussed objectively and which are open to criticism and verification. They are not formed by social scientists at random without check or restraint. The laws of their formation are very rigid and the scope of arbitrariness of the social scientist is much narrower than it seems at first sight. We are unable to enter into this problem here. But we will briefly summarize what has been presented elsewhere.[77]

1. Postulate of relevance. The formation of ideal types must comply with the principle of relevance, which means that the problem, once chosen by the social scientist, creates a scheme of reference and constitutes the limits within which relevant ideal types might be formed.

2. Postulate of adequacy. Each term used in a scientific system referring to human action must be so constructed that a human act performed within the life-world by an individual actor in the way indicated by the typical construction would be reasonable and understandable for the actor himself as well as for his fellow-man.

3. *Postulate of logical consistency.* The system of ideal types must remain fully compatible with the principles of formal logic.

4. *Postulate of compatibility.* The system of ideal types must contain only scientifically verifiable assumptions, which have to be fully compatible with the whole of our scientific knowledge.

These postulates give the necessary guarantees that the social sciences do in fact deal with the real social world, the one and unitary life-world of us all, and not with a strange world of fancy that is independent of and has no connection with our world of everyday life.

Concluding Remark [Ed.]

To go into further details of the typifying method seems to me one of the most important tasks of a theory of action. It is the great merit of Professor Parsons' work to have developed the principles and outstanding features of such a theory of social action and to have proved, at the same time, that the most famous masters of European social science have used this theory in their systems and have more or less explicitly set forth its basic principles and methods. Professor Parsons himself declares he is convinced that his book is not an end but a beginning of further research in the field of the theory of action. The preceding pages are written with the intention rather of continuing the discussion of these principles of social science than of criticizing the great work Professor Parsons has performed.

PART II

The Schutz-Parsons Letters
January 16, 1941 to April 21, 1941

Parsons: *"We seem to be unable to have a meeting of minds."* (January 16, 1941)

Dear Dr. Schutz:

At last I am ready to attempt a discussion of your long, and I think rather difficult, commentary on my book. I don't think it will be possible to cover the whole thing in one letter, even though it be a long one, but I shall attempt at least to make a pretty good start today and then carry it further within a few days.

After pretty careful consideration, I must say that I am unable to consider that your critical analysis necessitates any far-reaching revision of my own work, although in certain respects it points in directions in which my own thinking has already been moving. Indeed, there were a number of points at which I felt that reference to my later manuscript, a copy of which you have, would have helped clear up the points at issue. There are perhaps, if I may attempt to state them schematically in advance, three main reasons of a general character why I don't feel that your essay, taken in general terms, constitutes the kind of valid criticism the only adequate response to which would be a thorough-going reconstruction of the work it deals with. What is probably the least important of the three is that at certain points I feel you have definitely, sometimes seriously, mis-

Note: Letter headings and paragraphs have been introduced in order to facilitate the reader's orientation. Cross-references to the essay and letters are those of the authors themselves, except that pagination refers to this volume.—*Ed.*

understood my own argument. This is probably at least partly my fault, since my statements have doubtless often not been sufficiently clear. There is, however, one case where the misunderstanding is nothing short of glaring. On page 20 of your manuscript you refer to a statement that "when the advance from description and unit analysis to element analysis is made, it turns out that the action categories are not analytically significant." The statement was made in a footnote on page 762 of the book. You interpret this as applying to the status of action categories generally, whereas the statement itself in its context quite clearly refers only to their status in a *positivistic* system. When I read your statement I immediately felt that I could not have said such a thing on the general level on which you interpret it, and verification in my own text brought out the fact that it was very definitely a misunderstanding. I may or may not have been correct in maintaining that this was the case for a positivistic system but not for a "voluntaristic" system, but there can be absolutely no question of the meaning of my statement and it is definitely a critical error on your part not to have taken it as such.

There are other points which I felt also involved misunderstanding, notably when it comes to the relation between the concrete and abstract levels of use of the action schema, on the one hand, and the distinction between unit and element analysis on the other. You seem definitely to identify them in such a way the concrete level employs unit analysis, the analytical level element analysis. I am not sure that this can be pinned down to any one textual reference. This is quite definitely an interpretive error, and the two distinctions are independent of one another. Another point, a little later on, is your imputation to me of the view that the actor insofar as he acts rationally is *exclusively* oriented to the scientific verifiability of his knowledge of the situation. This also is a definite misunderstanding, and in so doing you set up a straw man who can, of course, quite easily be demolished. I shall return to this point later.

The second general comment is that we seem to be unable

to have a satisfactory meeting of minds because our foci of interest in these problems are quite different. I found myself marking at a number of points statements of yours which imply that my book was, along with the secondary examination of the work of other people, primarily a study of the methodology and epistemology of social science. On the very first page of your manuscript you refer, at the bottom, to my purpose of demonstrating that the four men converged on certain fundamental postulates of this methodology and epistemology. This statement seems to me symptomatic of a point of view which runs throughout your treatment. I think it is fair to say that you never carefully and systematically consider these problems in terms of their relation to a generalized system of *scientific theory.* It is this, not methodology and epistemology, which was quite definitely the central focus of my own interst. This difficulty seems to me most conspicuous in your discussion of the role of normative orientation and values. This aspect of my own treatment was very definitely worked out in terms of the problem of theoretical systematization, and that point of view I at least meant to be dominant through the work.

This is, naturally, not to say that considerations of methodology, and even at some points of epistemology, are irrelevant. There are a great many points at which such considerations had to be dealt with, but I still feel that the perspective in which they are treated is very greatly dependent on their relation to the problems of the status of a generalized system which includes a continual emphasis on the specific logical structure of the system and not merely on the status of certain of the conceptual elements which make it up. I think I can show how taking account of this would have forced you to change your position in many specific points. The general impression, however, is that you are simply not interested in what I call theory as distinct from methodology, and that your thinking does not run in those lines. In a sense, this is, of course, a matter of interpretation, but a much more generalized and subtle aspect of it than those I called attention to above.

The third general impression is, I think, related to these other two. It is that at a great many points you are interested in certain ranges of philosophical problems for their own sake which, quite self-consciously and with specific methodological justification, I have not treated. You are, for instance, continually attempting to point out certain things about what the subjective processes of action really are in what must be taken as a directly ontological sense. At another point you speak of the problem of ultimate value, again in a strictly philosophical sense. It is, I think, a corollary of my concentration of interest on a system of theory that I have attempted to minimize discussion of, and commitment to positions on, this philosophical level as much as possible.

In the first chapter of the book I tried to state in general terms my attitude toward the relations of scientific theory and philosophy. A critic is, it seems to me, entitled to do one of two things. He may radically question the general position I have taken and maintain, for instance, that for a scientific conceptual scheme to enjoy any sort of validity it must assume a kind of ontological status which I refuse to grant it. If, on the other hand, he does not wish to do this, he may attempt to show in detail that proper consideration of certain specific philosophical problems would alter the specific treatment of specific theoretical issues in specific ways.

From this point of view your treatment seems to me seriously unsatisfactory. You do not attack my general position in general terms, and yet in detail you do not seem to accept it, but again and again make statements which would imply that it was not tenable. When it is a matter of specific detailed considerations, however, you generally argue in the main that my general methodological attitude toward these is unsatisfactory, but you altogether fail to show how a different position would affect the actual logical structure of theory and its empirical use. I lay special emphasis on the latter. I think it is significant that there is not, in your whole essay, a single reference to the treatment of any empirical problem, for instance, in the work of any one of the four men. I regard it as perhaps the most important single merit of my book that it has not treated considerations of theory and methodology simply in terms of abstract generalities, but always in terms of their relation to specific and definite problems of the interpretation of empirical phenomena and generalization about such phenomena.

Again and again, in reading your work, you make points which as they are stated sound perfectly plausible, but I am always compelled to ask the question 'what of it?' If I accept your statement in place of my own formulations which you criticize, what *difference* would it make in the interpretation of any one of the empirical problems that run through the book, or in the formulation of the systematic structure of theory. I am certainly not prepared to say that in no case would they make any difference, but there is certainly not a single case in your essay where you *demonstrate* that it would, or what the difference would be. It seems to me an altogether legitimate requirement of criticism of a scientific work that the critic should show the importance of his criticism on this level. Again, there is no reason why the order of criticism which you make should not be important, but it seems to me both that it is an obligation on your part to show that it is important, and that if you attempted to do this you would be forced to put your analysis in the kind of perspective which I feel is seriously lacking throughout. Here again I have special reference to the question of relevance to a system of theory treated in terms of its specific usefulness in the understanding of certain quite definite empirical problems.

Having attempted to sum up my general impressions under these three heads, I shall at least begin to run through the particular points as they arise in the course of your discussion. The first point touches the definition of fact. This is one of the many points where usage, even among sophisticated scientists, is inconsistent. Facts are sometimes treated as part of our knowledge of the world, sometimes as aspects of the world of which we have knowledge. Surely the distinction between the content of knowledge, which is a system of interrelated propositions, and the things to which those propositions refer is elementary and fundamental. The limitation of the term fact to one of the two categories is in a sense arbitrary, but the kind of arbitrariness which is in the interests of clarity.

This elementary consideration seems to me distinct from the further problem of the relation between the structure of propositions and our experience of the external world. Your argument seems to presuppose that there is a kind of distinction between (1) that which is originally given in experience, (2) the interpretation of this given material, and (3) statements about this. I think these distinctions, while they are valid for certain purposes, are apt to be unrealistic. Actually the role of the conceptual scheme is only analytically distinguishable from given experience. We always observe, i.e. we experience, in terms of a conceptual scheme. Furthermore, precisely because and insofar as experience is conceptualized it is a matter of statements or propositions. I do not mean to say that verbal or other symbolic statements exhaust the full concreteness of experience, but those elements of experience which are crystallized and communicated are precisely those which are formulated in statements, at least so far as science is concerned. Hence, from the subjective point of view, knowledge of that aspect of experience which is crystallized in a certain form *consists of* systems of propositions. I simply cannot see any question of confusing these propositions with the phenomena to which they refer, and your critical statement that such a confusion runs through my book is entirely unconvincing to me. You give no actual examples where important conclusions seem to turn on such a confusion.

You make the statement toward the bottom of your third page that in the natural sciences facts can be described and classified without recourse to the "genealogy", whereas social facts cannot. (Note a terminological question: to me, *facts* are not "described" but are "stated".) This is, of course, on a certain level a correct observation. I cannot,

however, accept your inference from it. The principal difference on one level seems to me to be that so many of the
observed phenomena relevant to social science are treated
as symbols with meanings, whereas this conceptual scheme
is never used in physics. But in order to understand a system of symbols one must "know the language". This seems
to me to be the principal basis of the necessity for putting
any particular fact in a certain kind of broader context in
our field which is not necessary in the physical sciences. The
question of the demarcation line between common sense
interpretation of social facts and scientific statements
seems to me a matter of refinement rather than of basic
methodological principle.

I shall come back to this question in discussing your treatment of rationality. Shortly after this, however, it seems to
me that you make one of your most serious misinterpreta-
tions. On pages six and seven you state that the critical
remarks made in discussing the definition of fact may be
fully applied to the definition of a norm as a description of
course of action and then go on to speak of my tendency to
substitute statements for the phenomenon they deal with.
The question of the status of norms is a wholly different one
from that of the factual element in knowledge. This will be
a most important question for later discussion. The reason
for laying stress on the verbal description of a course of
action is precisely that a norm is, from the point of view of
the actor, a subjectively meaningful thing. It is, or is part
of, a "Sinnzusammenhang" in Weber's sense on a level
which is, for scientific purposes, most conveniently formulated in terms of symbols.

I have discussed at some length, especially in relation to
Pareto, the relation between such verbalizations and the
underlying "value attitudes" or sentiments which in a sense
they "express." This is certainly not a simple problem, but
the sense in which a verbalized norm expresses a value
attitude is quite radically different from that in which a
statement of fact describes an aspect of a phenomenon. The
referents of the linguistic symbols in the first case are sub-

jective entities, in the second aspects of the external world. From the observer's point of view value attitudes may be referred to as phenomena, though not in a concrete sense, but not from the point of view of the actor.

Since this brings us to the end of your most general methodological remarks, I think I had better stop here for the present. I quite realize that I have not yet adequately documented my general critical impressions. I shall, however, attempt to continue within a few days and I think will be in a position to build up a very considerable amount of evidence to back these general statements.

Sincerely yours,
Talcott Parsons

P.S. I have formulated my remarks somewhat sharply. No personal animus is intended, of course. I merely wish to further the clarity of discussion.

Schutz: *"A line to acknowledge receipt."* (January 21, 1941)

Dear Professor Parsons:

Just a line to acknowledge receipt, last Saturday, of your letter of 16th.

I think it would be best to wait with my answer until I have carefully studied your long and interesting letter and until I receive the second part you promised to send me. Of course I would understand fully if you would take time for such a work.

With kindest regards, I am

Sincerely yours,
Alfred Schutz

Parsons: *"I find nothing in your argument to shake my position."*
(January 23, 1941)

Dear Dr. Schutz:

I shall now attempt to proceed with my running comment on your paper, raising the problems as they arise in your own discussion. In outlining the principal features of the utilitarian system, I should like to make one or two comments. The problem of defining efficiency is exceedingly complex and I think that in the later manuscript you have seen I have gotten somewhat further with it than in the book. The most important point seems to me that verifiability in terms of empirical science is only one component of the total norm. The other most important one is minimization of cost, which can, I think, be shown to involve a reference to the total action system of the individual. This is hence one of the most important points at which the abstractness of the unit act becomes evident. Taking account of it would, I think, considerably modify your critical remarks later on about the difficulty of defining the unit act relative to wider complexes of action.

In the statement of what is meant by empiricism you have made a curious error of interpretation. The role of scientifically valid knowledge is taken account of in defining rational efficiency. By empiricism I meant something totally different—namely, the failure to take account of the abstractness of a conceptual scheme, in this instance, the tendency to treat the elements explicitly formulated in utilitarian theory as exhaustively descriptive of real concrete action.

When, on page 17 you speak of the introduction of an ultimate value system as the distinguishing characteristic of the voluntaristic theory, this is only correct in a very relative sense. It is that which most sharply distinguishes that system from the positivistic type. In other contexts quite different features might become the differentiating element.

Generally speaking, your summary of my argument seems reasonably adequate up to about page 19. There emerges again the difficulty I called attention to in my previous letter—your tendency to identify the distinction between concrete and analytical level on the one hand with that between unit and element analysis on the other. It is not, as you state in the middle of page 20, necessarily as a framework on analytical elements that the action scheme takes on a different meaning from that which it has as a descriptive scheme. On the contrary, I regard the system of theory which has emerged from the book as a whole not as a system of elements but rather of structural categories. This is why I gave the book the name *The Structure of Social Action,* and I have explicitly stated this at a number of points. I may call attention again to the fact that it is on page 20 that you have made this entirely unjustified statement that the action categories on the element level are not analytically significant.

The real difficulties begin later, however. On page 22 I may call attention to what seems to me a typical remark of yours, when you say "secondly, the attempt is made to unify their methodological remarks into a great system of theory." I think that is definitely inaccurate as a description of my procedure. I have not been primarily concerned with drawing the implications of the *methodological* remarks of the writers as such, but rather of elucidating their *theoretical* conceptual schemes in terms of their relation to empirical problems. The methodological discussion, which is important, is logically subordinated to this primary task. Another typical statement occurs on the same page where you impute to me the view "that all true description already necessarily presupposes a theoretical insight into the es-

sence of human activity." Taken in conjunction with repeated use of the terms "real" and "really" in your later
discussion, it seems to me justified to infer that you mean
"essence" in an ontological sense. I should like emphatically
to repudiate any claim to have advanced a theory of the
essence of human activity on this level. The question will
arise again repeatedly.

To me, one of the most unsatisfactory sections of your
discussion is the section on the concrete and analytic levels.
I feel that on this whole question you have misunderstood
me quite fundamentally. I am furthermore inclined to think
that the primary reason why you have misunderstood me is
your complete failure to think in terms of the logic of theoretical systems. What I mean by the analytic level is the set
of logical considerations that are involved in the statement
of the problem of determination of the state of a system as
a whole. It is the level that is presupposed in the statement
of a system of differential equations in mechanics. Confusion of this level with that which I call the concrete level is
a source of difficulty of the first importance in the history
of the theory of action. I should like above all to call attention in this connection to my treatment of the development
of Durkheim's conceptual scheme. The group mind difficulty in my opinion arose primarily because of Durkheim's
attempt to use a conceptual scheme which had been formulated in terms of what I call the concrete level as a basis of
generalization about the determination of a total system of
action. If you follow that analysis of Durkheim's work in
Chapters 9 and 10 carefully I do not see how you can fail to
get this point because it is absolutely central to the argument. Let me repeat that this question is logically quite
independent of the distinction between unit and element
analysis.

Another very curious statement of yours is that on page
25 that I obviously assume that the *concept* of the unit act
does not deal exclusively with universals. Of course, the
unit act is nothing but a combination of universals just as
the particle in mechanics is; but any particular act, just as

any particular particle such as the sun is not a universal but is the referent of a combination of specific statements of fact which, however, are stated in terms of the logical universals which compose the theoretical concept. I should like also to call attention to the fact that the same concepts may be treated as analytical elements or variables on the one hand, and as structural categories on the other, according to the way in which they are used.

Finally, though you say it is obvious, I cannot see the shift in the meaning of the term subjective point of view when applying it to element analysis and to unit analysis. This interpretation seems to me to depend entirely on the identification of this distinction with that of the two levels, which I have already stated was illegitimate. The facts in both cases are propositions which constitute the particulars corresponding to generalized categories of the theoretical system. Of course, they always refer to what are in some sense concrete, that is empirical, persons or pluralities of persons. Moreover, in some sense they always refer to aspects of the states of mind of those persons. According to the scientific problem in hand and the way in which it is treated, however, the character of the abstraction may differ in certain respects, but certainly there is no single obvious shift of meaning. Above all—you may argue the analytical level is abstract, not ontologically real—later you speak of fiction. But neither is the "concrete" level ontologically real. Neither, of course, is fiction. (Cf. my criticism of Weber on that point.)

I now come to the important question of the applicability of my standards of rationality to what we may call commonsense action. The most important point here seems to me to be that you persistently impute to me a quite false and untenable position—namely, that I hold that action is rational only in so far as it is *exclusively* determined by scientific knowledge. There may be certain of my formulations that are open to that interpretation, but I am perfectly certain that this is not possible for the argument of the book taken as a whole.

Exactly the contrary—it was my intention to show again
and again that it makes sense to speak only of rational
elements in action and never of action determined by reason
alone. I think I have many times stated that *all* the elements in the generalized sense which are involved in a total
system of action are involved in any particular act. Though
appearing at many points, this general position is perhaps
brought out most clearly in the discussion of Pareto. I may
make a few further comments on this. Of course, the common-sense actor has only partial knowledge and what he
has has not been formulated *primarily* from a scientific
point of view. But I have explicitly stated that it is not
statement in scientific form but verifiability by scientific
procedure which is the relevant criterion. Furthermore, I
have laid in the book very considerable stress on the importance of precisely the limitations on adequacy of knowledge.
You say the actor has a partial knowledge. In some cases,
however partial, this knowledge is adequate for his goals. In
other cases, however full, it is inadequate. The question of
adequacy of knowledge is one of the basic ones and I see no
possibility whatever of any approach to it in your terms.

I doubt, furthermore, whether there is any such thing as
a tenable "subjective concept of truth" which adequately
describes the logic of common-sense action but which is
different from that of science. My insistence on the continuity of the basic categories of logic and observation on the one
hand in the most sophisticated science, on the other hand
in the most simple common-sense action, is fundamental to
my whole position. You state that this is a philosophically
naive identification. That is your opinion. I find nothing in
your argument to shake my position. I can assure you that
I have thought it through exceedingly carefully from a
great many different points of view and though it is possible
that it is wrong, I think that I can say with considerable
confidence that it is not naive.

I tried to discuss this with you last year in relation to the
example of medical practice, and you seem entirely to have
missed my point in that discussion. I think I have gone very

considerably further with these problems since completion of the book, but I think it is also relevant that far from further consideration of them changing my opinion on this issue, it has served strongly to confirm it. I agree that the actor, as you say, is "not interested in the quest of certainty" though I should think your statement somewhat too absolute. Surely he is, however, primarily interested in other things. That, however, does not prove the irrelevance of scientific standards of verifiability. It proves only that the interest of the actor is not *confined* to the scientific truth of his beliefs. You say, on page 29, "he doesn't intend to find the scientific truth but only to check his private chances for success." This is an altogether unreal antithesis. How can he judge his chances of success without any judgment of the truth of the considerations on which his forecasts turn?

Let me take a contemporary political example. Mr. Roosevelt, we may assume, is interested in helping Great Britain prevent a decisive German victory. Surely, in the judgment as to what should or should not be done, it is highly relevant for him to attempt to know the truth about, for instance, the relative air strength of the British and the Germans and the corresponding probability of German's being able to break down British resistance before substantial American aid can become effective. To say that Mr. Roosevelt is not interested in the truth of these matters seems to me utterly incomprehensible. Of course, he is not interested in the truth for its own sake, but whether or not the reports he receives are reliable is surely of the very first importance.

On a smaller scale, I think substantially the same is true of all action which can be fitted into the rational means-ends context at all. I simply do not see how chances and risks can be weighed apart from the question of verifiability of knowledge. Perhaps most important of all, I cannot accept your drastic contrast between the point of view of the actor in the process of making decisions and retrospectively in interpreting past action. Certainly some important limitations on rational appraisal in the first case are absent in the second. But to state that the verifiability of propositions is irrelevant to the process of decision is to me entirely out of the question.

Let me take the case you give in your footnote: "The patient is not interested primarily in the scientifically correct treatment ordered by the physician, provided the treatment gives him a chance of health" (n. 51). I notice there you qualify the statement by using the word "primarily." In one sense I would agree. The patient certainly is not, apart from its bearing on his recovery, interested in the scientific understanding of his particular disease for its own sake, but he is surely overwhelmingly interested in the competence of his physician, and the whole structure of medical practice in our society is witness, and I state this with the greatest emphasis, that it is utterly impossible to divorce any standard of medical competence from considerations of the relative adequacy of scientific understanding of the diseases he is called upon to treat. Certainly there are differences in the system of relevance and interests, but these differences do not affect the basic points at issue.

Your argument on this whole question has completely failed to convince me. I have a very strong feeling that you have seriously misunderstood my position and have tended to criticize it in terms of a set of problems which is radically different from that involved in my work. Many of the things you say are quite tenable if they are taken as something other than criticisms of my work, but as criticisms they are, in my opinion, overwhelmingly either wrong or irrelevant.

Unfortunately I have no time to carry the discussion further into the question of normative value. My objections to your position there are at least as serious as they are in relation to the problem of rationality but I shall have to postpone their statement until a later time.

Sincerely yours,
Talcott Parsons

P.S. I think one more letter will complete my comment. I hope to send it next week.

Parsons: *"I must confess to being skeptical of phenomenological analysis."* (February 2, 1941)

Dear Dr. Schutz:

I shall continue and attempt to finish up this time my comment on your paper. I think possibly it will not be necessary to be quite so detailed from now on as certain main things should be coming out by this time.

I think I had better make a few remarks on your treatment of normative values and motives before coming to what is the most central point of all—that is, the relations of the objective and subjective points of view. You develop two possible interpretations of my use of normative elements in action. The second of them can, I think, be immediately repudiated. As you say, according to it no act is conceivable which is not at least *"wertrational."* To me the element of tension between rationality and any other norms and elements of action which oppose conformity with them is fundamental. The only thing I would want to remark beyond this in this connection is that the problem of integration of the total action system of an individual is logically distinct from the problem of defining the elements of a unit act. One of the most important sources of irrationality lies in defects of integration, which in turn have many different causes. Hence I do not think it legitimate to infer such a general proposition as that no irrational act would be conceivable without taking up the question of integration systematically.

My main concern, however, is with your first interpretation. There is clearly something radically wrong there. Part of it is a matter of the point I have already mentioned, failure to discriminate the two levels of analysis. I agree that there is a difference between what you call "a purely autonomous teleological" element and a "heteronomous command." I do not, however, agree that on the analytical level there is no difference between the latter and situational conditions or needs.

This whole problem was, I think, very thoroughly analyzed with special reference to Durkheim's treatment of it. It was precisely the confusion I am talking about which identified factual conditions of the situation with normative patterns which was the principal source of difficulty in Durkheim's early conceptual scheme, and more than anything else gave rise to the group mind problem. Furthermore, it was precisely by making the vital distinction that he finally solved his problem (in "L' éducation morale").

I am quite willing to grant that legal or other norms, once institutionalized, have a status for the concrete actor which is closely analogous to that of nonhuman conditions. Disobedience to these involves consequences beyond the control of the actor, the probability of which he must take into account. But this is a consequence of institutionalization and cannot be treated as a primary fact for analytic purposes without involving circular reasoning. This becomes perhaps particularly conspicuous when you include other-worldly sanctions as consequences of disobedience. Surely the automatic consequences of sin in the form of hell-fire, as conceived by a "hard-shelled" Baptist, are not of the same order as the consequences to an automobile driver of not keeping on the road.

I shall comment a little later on about some other aspects of the subjective point of view, but I think there is perhaps one other basis of difficulty here. Within certain limits it may well be true that the process of choice for a concrete individual between, as you say "means and ends ruled by a normative value" is very similar or even identical with his process of taking account of what are, in the analytical sense, situational factors. But my concern is not with the *psychology* of choice, but rather with the distinctions between and relations of elements in a social system. I do not hesitate to say that from this point of view it is utterly impossible to identify the two categories, and I think I have given a quite adequate analysis of why that is true. Let me here also call attention to your statement on page 32 about having to include in the value pattern the acts which Weber calls affectual and traditional. I say of course we must, and you may remember I discussed the reasons why value elements are included in those categories, as Weber uses them, at some length in my book. Exactly the same considerations apply to Pareto's concept of sentiments.

I now come to the question of motives, which is certainly a difficult one. It is true that I have not used the term 'motive' very much, but I wonder if, from one point of view, the argument is not very largely a verbal one. In the sense in which I should use the term a theory of motives is a central theme of the whole book. By that I should mean, though this is not a carefully considered definition, those elements in a system of action which are most closely analogous to forces in mechanics. It is implicit in the whole frame of reference I have used that these will be subjective entities. In detail, however, a generalized theory of the motivation of activity is an extremely complex thing, and I am quite sure that I made only certain beginnings in the book.

I feel that I have gone considerably farther in certain directions since then, as, for instance, in the article on Motivation of Economic Activity in the *Canadian Journal of Economics,* 6, 1940. But it is possible that you would refuse to call the things I deal with there motives at all. I very definitely do not consider that the treatment of motives is the exclusive business of psychology. From my point of view normative patterns, or values, are not *substitutes for* a theory of motives, but elements of a system of action which have to be *incorporated into* a theory of motives.

Coming to the distinction of the two types of motives, I

don't think that what you call the "in-order-to" motive leads to any difficulties. Indeed, it seems to me essentially what I mean by an end, a concept which overlaps with values. I should almost say that from my point of view the motive is not the future state of affairs but a subjective anticipation of such a state of affairs and that not all of the concrete anticipation could be accorded motivational significance, rather only those elements which on the one hand are desired, on the other hand would not come about without the agency of the actor. It seems to me that in any other than a verbal sense you cannot say that I have ignored this element of motivation. I have merely, it seems to me, used different terms, but the substance of what you call attention to is fully taken account of.

What you call the "because motive" is a source of far greater difficulty to me. I do not think I fully understand all its implications as you use it, but, generally speaking, two things seem to stand out. In the first place, I should not refer to any cognitive interpretation of past action as a motive. I should, on the contrary, treat it as part of the "definition of the situation" in W. I. Thomas's sense. There is, of course, a difficulty in that we cannot treat situations as simply given, but in understanding their relation to action we must know how they are defined by the actor. Elements of error, bias, and the like may well enter in and be important. I should not, however, refer to these elements as motives in the ordinary sense. They are, I think, also taken account of in my book, particularly in the parts dealing with Weber's Sociology of Religion, where rationalization of religious ideas is treated as having precisely this function of defining the situation in which motives act. The term 'motives' for this purpose would be very close to that of 'interests' as used by Weber.

The second problem that bothers me is how far your insistence on a difference between the project and the reflective interpretation of past action is of analytical significance for my purposes. I can grant the distinction without difficulty and I can certainly see certain limitations on precise and consistent formulation of projected goals which do not exist for "hind-sight." I suspect, however, that we are subject to very important bias in our interpretations of the past as well as the future, for instance with respect to the inevitability of what has already happened. Although I do not think I have fully grasped this part of your argument, I strongly suspect that considerations which I brought forward in connection with the discussion of rationality are applicable here. I think, that is, that what is to me your untenable antithesis between naive common sense and scientific knowledge is also involved here. I think there is a far closer relation between our meaningful interpretations of the future and the past than you seem to. In both connections there is, of course, enormous variation in precision, self-consciousness, and so on.

You surely cannot accuse me of not taking account of the fact that motives are organized in, as you say, "great subjective systems," since, precisely as distinguished from the utilitarian position, I have consistently emphasized the importance of this throughout. The question of what you speak of as "exclusively subjective systems" I shall postpone for a few moments. You say it is a merit of your position to avoid the metaphysical problem of ultimate value and ultimate aims. I am sure you have misunderstood here my use of these terms. The ultimacy is not a metaphysical plane but relative to the structure of a particular system of action. As I use the concepts I think it is perfectly clear that a metaphysical problem is not raised. The question of transition in the shift of relevance and attention does not, I think, raise serious difficulties for me. I am quite ready to grant that the system of motives exists in time. I am not, however, ready to grant that values or ends are significant only temporarily at a particular moment of the life process. The question of elements of stability of orientation on the one hand, of growth and more or less random shifting on the other, is certainly complicated, but both on the level of personality and of social structure there are certainly elements of continuity which your argument does not take account of. I radically deny that the conceptual scheme I have developed is applicable only to a certain given moment.

Finally, you state (on pp. 35–36) that the works of Durkheim, Marshall, Pareto, and Weber are interpretable as systems of motives in your sense. You do not, however, show by a single example how this is true, and above all, that interpreting them in that way would make *any difference* from the way in which I have interpreted them. This is to me a striking example of your tendency to avoid empirical problems. Surely, if there is any point at which you could show that taking account of your criticism would make a radical difference in my conclusions, this is one of the most favorable, but all you do is assert your analysis can be empirically applied. You do not attempt to do it.

Just a word about the question of the limits of the unit act. Generally speaking, your analysis is quite correct, above all the point that the unit act is not somehow a natural entity but that what is treated as a unit act is operationally relative to the problems in hand. I think I have emphasized that myself. The point at which I differ from you is your conclusion that somehow there is a natural or real subdivision of the continuous subjective stream such that if one really took account of the subjective point of view these questions would be automatically decided. I quite radically disagree with your view that the subdivisions of systems are in a natural sense present in the mind of the actor but are not accessible to the observer. There are unquestionably many cases where it is possible for an observer, with the proper skills and the opportunities, to know a great deal more about an actor in many respects than he can know about himself. Above all, what the actor does self-consciously know about himself is not somehow an immediate reflection of an ontological reality but is just as much mediated through a conceptual scheme and hence selected as to fact and selectively organized as what an observer knows about another.

If there is one thing which the experience of psychoanalysis, with the relations between the conscious ego, the unconscious, and pre-conscious, can be said to have proved it is this. A notable instance is the proof of the very high degree of selectivity of memory for experiences, particularly in childhood. Any process by which some and certainly never all of these limitations can be overcome is precisely the same kind of process as that by which a self-conscious scientist in his understanding of others overcomes the kinds of limitations which are inherent in common sense. Any kind of phenomenological reflection about one's own experience is, I think, in this respect on the same general level as the process of psychoanalysis. I certainly do not think it can give us a complete and unbiased picture of the subjective. It can only remove *particular* sources of bias and discover *particular* facts. The operational relevancy of the unit act seems to me essentially the same as that of units for other types of systems.

From a common sense point of view, of course, a physical body or, more technically, a particle, is simply a spatially distinct "thing", but for the technical purposes of mechanics a particle is anything relative to which certain operations can be carried out. We speak of the earth as a particle, and it is treated as such in the theory of the solar system, but we are wholly aware at the same time that it is "made up" of an indefinite number of distinct particles, and this process of sub-division can be carried out indefinitely. What is an act, what is the process of pursuing a given end or goal is not something which is ontologically given either to the observer or to the actor but is that sector of the phenomena which proves operationally convenient to treat as a unit for the purposes in hand.

There are two particular issues I should like to note here. In the middle of page 40 you state that "all this is open only to the knowledge of the actor himself . . . For the observer has no other access to the action of the actor but the acts once accomplished." I take it you mean physically observable overt acts. I beg to differ fundamentally. The observer has, in addition to the observation of overt acts, an enormously large accumulation of phenomena which we interpret as symbolic expressions of the actor's states of mind. Obviously the most important class of these are linguistic expressions of the most various sorts. It is not confined to language but includes all kinds of facial expressions and aspects of the context of action. Furthermore, a very large proportion of overt acts, such as ritual acts, are interpreted in the context of symbolic expression rather than in terms of means adapted to an end. The knowledge of a particular person's life which is involved in a psychoanalytic case history is only to a minimum degree composed of observations of the subject's overt acts. It is overwhelmingly a matter of interpretations of linguistic expressions, expressing sentiments, recounting memories, and the like. But even overt acts are not described and interpreted in terms of a physical frame of reference but of the frame of reference of action itself. This is one of the important points of Weber's concept of *"aktuelles Verstehen"*, where, you remember, he treated "reaching for the door-handle to shut the door," as a matter of *description,* not of interpretation of motives.

Closely related with this point is that of the different levels of abstraction on which we treat observation. As I shall point out presently, there is reason to believe we never come anywhere near exhaustive description of objective phenomena, but perhaps the closest approach to it is a complete psychoanalytic case history. It is not, however, necessary, in order to have valid knowledge of action, to have anything like this detailed knowledge of the personality and motives of each actor. On another level, one could have a sufficient detail in order to understand adequately the relatively concrete personal relationships between people involved in a particular situation—for instance, the members of a university department. On still another level, it is possible to treat certain aspects or sectors of the individual's life which are structurally significant without being in a position to say anything about particular motives in particular situations whatever. In my study of medical practice, for instance, I am able to say a good deal about the patterns governing the behavior of medical men without having

studied their particular relations in specific situations sufficiently to be able to diagnose those situations at all adequately. I think the situation is logically analogous to the
treatment of the behavior of celestial bodies in astronomy
without having studied the component bodies that make up
each planet or star.

The other point I wanted to bring out is your statement
on page 41 that the demarcation line between ends and
conditions of an act can be drawn only by the actor himself
because what the actor considers as means pertains really
to the conditions and vice versa. It is necessary, therefore,
in judging rationality to project the actor's knowledge on
the standard of the best available scientific knowledge. But
your formulation fails to take into account an essential
element of relativity in the situation. To take a medical
example—I have just been reading in the life of Sir William
Osler that Osler repudiated the use of the drugs known in
his time in the treatment of pneumonia and believed that
the disease must run its course. Since his time, a drug,
sulfapyridine, has been discovered which radically checks
the progress of pneumonia. I should not judge Osler irrational because he did not recommend the use of this drug.
Certainly a basic criterion is the knowledge an actor in a
given situation could be *expected* to possess. Naturally,
what this is is relative to the time and cultural situation.
Conversely, I should not take ability to detect errors in
commonly believed ideas which nobody in the situation of
the actor saw, as a criterion of rationality. It seems to me
this is a pragmatic difficulty such as that which arises in the
empirical use of any conceptual scheme and not at all, as
you treat it, an evidence of a basic shortcoming of the
scheme itself. I may also remark that I am quite sure that
I have treated the biological individual, the organism, as an
abstraction in exactly the same sense that the actor is an
abstraction.

We may now come to the question of the objective and
subjective points of view. I really think that I have finally
succeeded in straightening out the difference between us on

this question. I think what you mean essentially is an ontological reality, what a concrete real actor "really" experiences. I think I have legitimate reasons to be skeptical that
by your analysis or by any others available it is possible to
arrive at anything approaching a definitive description of
such a reality. I am afraid I must confess to being skeptical
of phenomenological analysis. But however that may be, I
mean something quite different.

I mean a set of categories for the description and analysis
of the empirical phenomenon of human action, a set of categories involving a frame of reference which has the same
order of significance and is put to the same kind of uses as
is a frame of reference in any empirical science. From my
point of view, the antithesis you draw between the objective
and subjective points of view is unreal. There is no such
thing as a body of knowledge or scientifically relevant experience which represents the "pure" subjective point of view.
Subjective phenomena have meaning *only* as described and
analyzed by an observer.

What is meant by subjective is, I think, the organization
of the relevant facts about a point of reference, which is as
characteristic of our field as the Cartesian "origin" is of
classical mechanics. Just as in classical mechanics any
statement of physical fact must be referred to one or more
bodies capable of location with reference to the origin in a
system of coordinates, so in the theory of action any statement of fact must be referable to one or more actors who are
units, not located in space, but having certain properties.
What these properties are is a matter of the specific "subjective categories" employed in the system—that is, actors
have goals, knowledge, beliefs, sentiments, and the like. The
frame of reference and the system of categories constitute
an articulate system, the outline of which in certain terms
I have tried to work out. The empirical facts stated, organized, and analyzed in terms of the system of categories are
always, in the logical nature of the case, facts observed and
stated by an observer. Their verifiability is always a matter
of operations performed relative to certain kinds of experi-

ence and objects of experience, notably what we call overt acts and symbolic expressions.

The process of reading this letter with a view to understanding what I mean is just as much an *operation* in the methodological sense as is the process of surveying a piece of land. What we mean by the "state of mind" of the actor is simply the unitary referent of certain possible statements of fact arrived at in this way. It is no more and no less an ontological reality than the particle of classical physics or the wave system of certain versions of quantum mechanics.

The question of reflective observation seems to me simply to introduce a certain complication. I think the various things you have said about the alter ego simply confirm my general view. It is true that we generally formulate the conceptual scheme in terms of an observer, A, observing and interpreting the actions of another actor, B. But this is not more essential than that the prototype of astronomical observation should be of an observer on the earth observing another body, the sun. It is quite possible for the observer on the earth to attempt to observe the corresponding properties of the earth itself, although there are certain technical difficulties involved. Actually his knowledge of those corresponding properties is largely obtained by observing the interrelations of corresponding properties on the earth with the properties of other bodies of a like nature.

Correspondingly, I think most of our self-knowledge is derived from our knowledge of our interrelations with other actors. But I see no reason to believe that the knowledge acquired by self-reflection is any closer to ontological reality than the knowledge acquired by observation of the action of others. Furthermore, I see every reason to believe that the basic conceptual schemes we use in the two cases are identical. There are methodological reasons for this but there are also very important empirical reasons involved in our knowledge of the process of socialization of the child and of the senses in which self-consciousness is a function of meaningful relations with others. I call your attention here to the works of Mead and of Piaget.

I fully agree with your argument about behaviorism. I do not think you intend to make me out as a behaviorist, but what you sketch on pages 46–48 is not, I think, my position either. I think the really important point is my radical questioning whether for purposes of science the kind of distinction you attempt to set up between this intermediate position and one which, as you put it, neglects what the social world means to the actors within it is essentially unreal. The position I take is certainly not that of certain schools of economic thought which restrict themselves to studying such things as indifference curves and claim thereby to have eliminated the concept of utility. That is something very close to behaviorism and I think ends up there if followed out consistently.

I insist continuously on the use of the subjective point of view, but in the form of subjective categories in a conceptual scheme and not in the form of an account of what the subjective social world "really" is. I think subjective categories in this sense are always involved in any description of social phenomena which does not reduce it to what are actually biological or physical terms. I certainly cannot accept your view that, of Znaniecki's four schemes, those of group and relation are objective and action and personality are subjective. From my point of view all four are *both* objective and subjective in exactly the sense that I have been trying to emphasize. Having stated this general point of view, it seems to me that the question becomes one of the specific detailed theoretical problems. I do not for a moment maintain that my formulations of these various things are definitive in any sense. They are certainly destined to be progressively modified and refined. My general feeling, however, is that you have not taken what is to me the fruitful path in carrying out the process of revision.

I should conceive it as a matter of showing how the careful and consistent use of this kind of category led to specific empirical and theoretical difficulties. The kind of thing I mean is illustrated, for instance, by the utter inability of classical mechanics to take account of the facts of radio–

activity. This discovery and various others led to a theoretical reconstruction with at least the negative result that on the microscopic level matter could not be conceived as a system of atoms if these were interpreted as particles in the sense of classical mechanics, and if their relations were those of bodies in motion in the same sense. I think I have been able to show in an analogous sense that certain of the facts of the development of a system of free enterprise, as they are stated and analyzed by Marshall, Durkheim, and Weber, are incompatible with the scheme which I have called the utilitarian system, which I think is even today to a very large extent embodied in our common-sense interpretations of these phenomena. It may well be that we already have the factual knowledge which is necessary to show that my own formulations of a theory of action are as obsolete as is classical mechanics for atomic research in the days of quantum theory. Only a long period of research and critical analysis can show.

All I can record is my personal conviction that you have not shown this in your own criticism. I am inclined to go farther and say that by the critical procedure you have adopted it would not be possible to show it even if the necessary facts were available. I don't think such a thing can be shown without detailed critical analysis of empirical problems. As I have said before at a number of points, I feel able to assent on general grounds to your non-critical formulations because they seem in accord with my own experience. I do not, however, see their relevance to what is my field of interest, the development of a systematic theoretical scheme for empirical use in the social field. Practically every statement of yours, so far as I have understood it, which might, if its implications were followed up, be relevant to that seems to me to rest upon inadequate understanding of my own argument.

This impression, which is naturally only a personal impression which is subject to error, is curiously confirmed by the last few pages of your development. After developing a critical point of view the logical implication of which would seem to be that a very radical revision of the whole thing would need to be undertaken, you end up with formulations which, so far as they go, I find entirely acceptable. Of course, it is a fact that the actual analytic concepts we use in dealing with mass phenomena are highly abstract relative even to the order of concreteness which is available to us in particular cases. Just as our knowledge of the sun is not a resultant of an examination in detail, one by one, of every atom that makes it up, so our knowledge of human behavior is not a resultant of detailed study of every human being who has ever lived. Once these steps in the direction of generalization and abstraction are made, you reach a level which seems to me fairly closely comparable to that on which most of my analysis proceeds.

The only important disagreement I think I have is in your limitation of concepts on this level to the ideal type. I have already in my book attempted to show in a great detail why this limitation is not acceptable, and I think now I should be able to go considerably farther. What you fail to show, however, is how the more general methodological considerations which occupy the bulk of your analysis bear on the use and formulation of concepts on this level, especially, as I must insist again, in a way which would lead to different results from my use. There is, from this point of view, simply a gap. All this leaves me wondering whether the whole argument is worth the trouble.

I think my whole attitude ends up in this dilemma, or shall I say trilemma? First, I incline to the view that, generally speaking, your discussion consists of two main elements:

(a) Criticisms based on inadequate understanding of my work, which are capable of being corrected by a more thorough study. I have attempted to document this fully.

(b) The introduction of considerations relative to the analysis of the subjective point of view from points of view rather different from my own which are not important to my own analysis in the very simple sense that taking account of them would not lead to important modifications.

Just as I have charged you with failure to understand *my* position adequately, it is quite possible that the principal source of the difficulty lies in *my* failure to understand *you*. I think I have given sufficient evidence above that this cannot be the whole story, but it may well be an important part of it; but if it is, there is still the further problem of whether on the one hand I have simply failed to understand a philosophical approach which is really concerned with quite different problems from mine, and on the whole, instead of criticizing each other we have simply been talking about different things. In so far as my own inadequacies are the cause of the difficulties, I am inclined to think that the explanation is more likely to run in this direction, since I have spent so many years exploring the ins and outs of my own system it seems scarcely credible that I should not be able to find the kind of meeting ground where we could really join issue in a fruitful way.

The final possibility, on the other hand, is that your argument runs along lines which I simply fail to understand but which, for reasons I again do not understand, really does vitiate the essentials of my own position. Anyone who is intellectually honest must reckon with the possibility of this being true. All I can say is that though it may be, I do not believe so, but will do my best to understand further evidence presented.

Sincerely yours,
Talcott Parsons

Schutz: *"I shall let you have my reaction soon."* (February 10, 1941)

Dear Professor Parsons:

Thank you ever so much for your third letter dated February 2nd, which I received February 8th.

Of course, I have to study your three letters carefully and I will answer them thoroughly after having examined all the points with the necessary care.

It may be that I shall not be able to send this answer for several weeks as I am for the time being very much occupied. Of course, I shall do my best to let you have my reaction as soon as possible.

Sincerely yours,
Alfred Schutz

Schutz: *"You have to go a few steps further in radicalizing your theory."* (March 17, 1941)

Dear Professor Parsons:

Having carefully studied the three long letters you have devoted to my paper I feel that I have to make a few statements which seem to me very important, first of all for personal reasons.

You start your comments with a resume of your general impressions of my paper and therefore I will perhaps be allowed to give you an account of my impressions of your reaction. Frankly speaking, I feel that you have unfortunately entirely misunderstood the spirit in which I wrote the paper—or better the draft for a future paper—which I ventured to submit to you. You have interpreted it exclusively as a criticism of your work and have not admitted that it also lays claim to being an independent contribution to the discussion of certain problems, on the clarification of which we have both spent many laborious years of our lives. You impute to me throughout, therefore, an antagonistic attitude toward your position, which I have not had at all. To be sure, there *are* criticisms of some of your theories in this paper, and I have never hesitated to make clear where I have to disagree with you. But it seems to me that the bulk of my paper shows where and in how far our theories coalesce.

This chief point has been entirely overlooked by you. No wonder then, that according to you "points (I) make sound as they are stated perfectly plausible," but that you are always compelled to ask the question "what of it?" or that many of the things I say "are quite tenable if they are taken as something other than criticisms of (your) work." I think we could find here the common meeting ground for further and more fruitful discussions, provided that you are interested in my problems in the same measure as I am in yours, and provided, furthermore, that you do not doubt the intellectual honesty of my arguments. I hope sincerely that you are convinced, if not of the relevance of my statements, then at least of the loyalty and fairness of my attitude toward you personally and toward your ideas. By nature and temperament I am always inclined to search in daily and scientific life for common bases of mutual understanding rather than merely to criticize. But if that were not the case, I feel I should have to adopt such an attitude at any rate in dealing with a man whose work I sincerely admire.

Let me remind you, therefore, of the genesis of my paper of which I told you when I had the pleasure of meeting you for the first time, and which, as far as I remember, I repeated in the letter accompanying my manuscript. Although I am a newcomer to this country, I think I am not a newcomer to the scientific field of the theory of action. My book, in which I developed a systematic theory of social action—as incomplete and open to criticism as it may be—was published in 1932. This book did not have the good fortune to provoke your attention. I regret this fact, above all because you would certainly not have made some basic objections to my principal position if you had ever accorded it your serious scrutiny. The principles of this book—which is the result of twelve years of conscientious research—are intergrated into a theoretical system of social action, which, to be sure, starts from a point of view other than your own, although it shares your aim of developing a theoretical scheme for empirical use.

Some English scholars—most of them belonging to the London School of Economics—considered my ideas interesting enough to have a summary of my system published in the *Economica* in 1937, inviting me at the same time to contribute a paper of my own in English. Afterwards your book appeared and was sent to me upon my request by American friends at the beginning of 1938. I studied it as carefully as the circumstances of my private life permitted, and I realized immediately the importance and the value of your system and also the fact that it starts exactly where my own book ends. Happy to find a work accessible to English readers and presenting, besides its own very important theories, an excellent discussion of Max Weber's sociology, I proposed to my friend, Professor Hayek, editor of *Economica,* that I should begin my paper on my own work with a presentation and discussion of your theory. Hayek agreed.

Different events have delayed the project but not my continuous study of your book. One year ago, when I had the pleasure of meeting you for the first time, I told you of the great difficulties I had been encountering in my endeavors to fully understand certain points of your system. We agreed that I should write down some questions in the form of critical remarks, which were to constitute, if I may say so, a program for future discussions. We agreed also that I should ask Hayek again whether he would keep his invitation open. You know his answer; he is willing to concede 5,000 words for the presentation of your as well as my ideas.

I spent the summer months of last year studying your book again and again. Entering more and more deeply into your problem, I found new and interesting points of convergence with and divergence from my own thoughts, and, as I meditated pen in hand, I put down not 5,000 but 25,000 words. This monster of a paper was of no use at all short of the clarification of my own thought. The only part which has been rewritten three times is the first one, which deals with the presentation of your thought. There I tried to retain your own wording and you have certainly observed that the first 18 pages are nothing other than an attempt at compiling the high-lights of your book in your own language. (This procedure of course, does not at all exclude or excuse all kinds of misunderstanding on my part.) Having finished, I was rather uncertain whether I had not better do the whole job over again. But I thought it would be more advisable to show you the manuscript in its present form in order to find a basis for discussing the several points in your theory, the meaning of which I could not see clearly enough. I thought that this would be the fairest and best way to clarify certain of my difficulties in the understanding of your work. I went even a step further. Rewriting chapter one I put in it some points which are not connected with the following argument and I did so only to provoke your reaction and to ascertain whether my interpretation of your thought was right or wrong. Although I explained it carefully in my letter with which I sent you the manuscript, this procedure of establishing a kind of "questionnaire" in the form of a criticism unfortunately did not win either your attention or your approval. You deal with my manuscript not as if it were a first draft of a presentation of your thought, submitted to the author personally and not to the public by an interested sympathizer seeking enlightenment, but as if I had published it as it is before consulting you. Otherwise, I could not understand several of your observations, for instance the one which I read at the end of page 1 and the beginning of page 2 in your first letter.

But enough of personal remarks! I think that what I have stated so far is self-explanatory and will thus, I hope, correct the ideas you may have formed concerning my intentions and the intentions of the manuscript in question. The fact that I have spent so many pages on the foregoing exploration may show you that it is very important to me to be understood by you—at least so far as our personal relations are concerned.

I turn now to the general comments contained in your first letter. As I explained before, I had neither expected nor intended to suggest by my critical analysis a far-reaching revision of your work. Feeling that I am in agreement with the greater part of your basic thought, I should only regret it if for one reason or another you felt induced to modify the basic tenets of your system. So, even if my so-called criticism were free of the faults which you find in it, I could not see any sufficient reason in my arguments for a thoroughgoing reconstruction of your work. And I stated several times in my paper—e.g., p. 22 and p. 60—that it is written with the intention of continuing the discussion of some principles of the social sciences, rather than of criticizing the great work you have performed.

The first defect you find in my paper is that I have definitely misunderstood some of your thoughts. I am not surprised to hear that this is the case, as one principal aim of my paper was the clarification of some of my interpretations. You know certainly that your book makes no easy reading, even for scholars whose mother tongue is English and who have been brought up in the Anglo-American tradition. So it may be that I frequently could not see your meaning clearly. But some of my "misstatements" have their origin in real ambiguities in the wording of your ideas, others in my endeavors to provoke your reaction in order to clarify my own thoughts.

The latter is the case when I quoted the footnote on page 762 of your book and accepted the interpretation that it turns out, in the advance from description and unit analysis to element analysis, that the action categories are not analytically significant. It seems that this quotation has aroused your special indignation, and you react as if I had imputed to you with deliberate malice pure nonsense with the sole purpose of criticizing it thereafter. To be sure, I was not at all convinced in putting down this quotation as to whether you had the intention of pretending that the action category drops out on a certain level of theoretical discussion. If you will do me the favor of reading again and without prejudice pp. 762 to 764 first paragraph in your book, you will certainly acknowledge that the text is at least equivocal. The great difficulty, I feel, consists in the relation between *cultural* systems and action. I agree fully with you that cultural systems may be considered as *products* of processes of action. But these systems of culture furnish the best example of a field open to element analysis where the action categories are not analytically significant. I think that the same can be asserted quite generally for all products of human action. I *can* always consider them in terms of the action frame of reference, but there is an analytical level where the action element drops out, and that is always the case if I am examining the products of action as such, without including in my scope the acts which produced them.

In my different writings I personally made myself a defender of this thesis, which you seem now definitely to reject. All action sciences, that is my thesis, may reach an analytical level, where they deal exclusively with the objects constituted by and through acts of an actor without considering the actor and his acts or, in other words, by dropping the action categories themselves. If this is true, and I think it is, it would of course not make any difference what kind of action theory—a positivistic or a voluntaristic one—were to be adopted, as no action theory at all would be required for this specific level of analysis. That is my opinion, and I hoped that my quotation of your footnote would provoke you into telling me if you share this view or not. Unfortunately the latter is the case. For all the following arguments in my paper, however, this point is without relevance, as none of them is based on this issue, however important it may be for me in some other direction.

My second chief misunderstanding according to your first letter is my identification of unit analysis with the concrete level and element analysis with the analytical level. You declare that this is definitely an interpretive error on my part and that the two distinctions are independent of each other. I frankly declare that if both unit analysis and element analysis are applicable on both levels, the concrete and the analytical, I have misunderstood your theory in an essential point. But the consequence is that I can no longer see any difference between the functional significances of these two levels which you distinguish. Even if I could imagine how a unit analysis could be performed on the analytical level—I would suppose that this would be the case if an ideal-typical act were analyzed by showing the typical unit-elements involved, and among them a typical actor—I cannot see at all how an element analysis could be applied to a so-called concrete act. Or am I to understand that you will accept with the statement of the mutual applicability of both forms of analysis to both levels of abstraction, only *my* statement on p. 25, namely, that element analysis as well as unit analysis can be performed on each level of concreteness? But then we should have to discuss carefully what you understand by the term "level," which in my opinion depends exclusively on the analytical methods applied to it.

Concerning the third misunderstanding quoted by you at the beginning of your first letter, I cannot see that I imputed to you the view that the actor acting rationally is *exclusively* oriented to the scientific verifiability of his knowledge of the situation. On the contrary, I quoted on pp. 17 and 18 some of your statements (p. 81 cf. your book) that this is not your opinion. Nevertheless, the statement that the action is rational only if the actor acts for reasons understandable and verifiable by positive empirical science constitutes an integral element of your definition of rationality, and if rationality is not defined solely by reference to reasons verifiable by positive science, there is, according to your definition, obviously no rationality at all if such verifiability is entirely lacking.

Your second general comment on my paper is that our problems are quite different, as you are interested first of all in a generalized system of scientific theory whereas you feel that I am primarily studying methodological and epistemological problems. I do not think that such a difference really does exist between our goals and I feel quite strongly that there is here a difference in terminology—rather than in thought.

I fear that in this country the terms methodology and epistemology are used in a more restricted sense than their equivalents in German and I accepted these terms only because I could not find any better translation for "Wissenschaftslehre" which includes both logical problems of a scientific theory and methodology in the restricted sense. I consider that your book as well as mine (and even my paper) deals with such problems of a "Wissenschaftslehre" of the social sciences and that, for instance, a discussion concerning the subjective point of view in the action scheme is as integral a part of the scientific theory of the social world as anything else. To my mind, of course, the term "methodology" has no limitative meaning and certainly not at all a pejorative one. And I am the first to acknowledge that one of the great merits of your study consists in building up a "Wissenschaftslehre" of the social sciences starting from specific and definite problems of the interpretation of empirical phenomena and generalizations thereof. Moreover, I think that the chief topic of both studies—yours and mine —has been and is to outline the theoretical system of the fundamental science of the social world, namely the science of social action.

This leads me to your third general remark, the relation between philosophy and such a theory of the social world. May I be allowed to make here an autobiographical comment. I did not start my scientific endeavors as a philosopher or logician although these problems had always evoked my deepest interest since my undergraduate days. I came from the most concrete problems of economics and of the theory of law. But I recognized early that the theoretical systems of those disciplines cannot be built up scientifically without entering into a scientific study of the structure of the social world, and that means of the general theory of social action. On the other hand, I found that only a very few scholars, for instance Max Weber and Pareto, had even posed these problems in a sufficiently radical way and that even these men had to prepare specific logical tools of their own. My great admiration for the work performed by these scholars did not prevent me from recognizing some of their basic tenets as unsufficiently clarified and sometimes as incompatible with certain results of modern philosophy and logic. That is why I turned to Bergson's and Husserl's philosophy, hoping to find there the tools for working in the field of the most concrete problems of social sciences, and I personally must say that my expectations have not been disappointed. I have been continuously trying to check my results by applying them to the most concrete problems of the social sciences and have had the satisfaction of seeing that my way of thinking has proved helpful for some of my friends in their daily scientific work. I mention this just to show that I have not been and am not an ontological dogmatist, and I think that no reader of my book could come to such a conclusion.

But, of course, I insist that any statement made in the field of social theory has to be at least consistent with and explicable by means of the whole body of well-established philosophical knowledge.

Now I have to respond to your argument that I must not promulgate other solutions without showing how a different position would affect the actual logical structure of your theory and its empirical use. First of all, this argument would be applicable only if my paper was intended to be nothing but a criticism of your book, whereas, as stated above, it is meant first of all as a discussion of some basic problems of our science from a different point of view. Secondly, you cannot request me to enter into a detailed discussion within the frame of a paper already overburdened with other topics. I shall be glad, of course, to treat this subject, if you want me to do so, in an oral discussion and I hope to give you some comments you might be interested in.

But all this does not reach the core of the problem. You say that I do not attack your general position in general terms and yet in details I do not seem to accept it but make again and again statements which would imply that it was not tenable. I thought I had explained my point of view sufficiently in my paper.

May I sum it up as follows: I accept your basic position as such and in so far as I, like you, am convinced that a general theory of social science has to be based on a careful analysis of unit acts and a theory of the structure of social action, and this from the subjective point of view. I accept, furthermore, your respective analyses insofar as they might be sufficient for the treatment of the chief problems within the limits you have chosen for the book under examination.

On the other hand, I think that your analyses are not radical enough first of all as far as the subjective point of view is concerned and that you take for granted many phenomena which need further examination. As examples I want to state that nowhere in your own theory do you deal with the specific *social* categories of acting and mutual interaction, with the problem of the frame of reference relative to the alter ego towards which the actor's own actions are oriented and within which the alter ego interprets the actor's action; that all your statements concerning the structure of the act are applicable as well to the act of the solitary actor as to the act oriented towards and motivated by an alter ego; that, consequently, you have disregarded the vital importance of the time element in all human action and the differences between the logical significance of an act already performed and an act just projected and, on the other hand, the categories of personality and anonymity; that, in particular, you do not explain the specific attitude the social scientist has to adopt towards the social world, which is an attitude derived from that of the partner in the social world, but with quite other "operational signs" or "subscripts" which bestow in both cases a different meaning upon any interpretation of an alter ego's act; that hence your theory of values as well as the role you attribute to science is acceptable only if you forego the explanation of the problems of intersubjectivity involved in both and if you presuppose the whole social world with all its structural differentiations just as given, allowing "values" and "science" to enter your system $\theta \acute{\upsilon} \rho \alpha \theta \epsilon \nu$ "through the door" if I may use this Aristotelian term.

All these questions can be clarified by a radical analysis of social intersubjectivity. Of course you might object that you are not interested in those problems, and that you do not consider them to be problems of a theory of action. Against such an objection I would be defenseless. I, personally, have been and am above all interested in them and believe that a full understanding, for instance, of the so-called subjective and objective point of view can be gained only by entering courageously into this far too little explored realm. Furthermore, I feel that only such a study would be able to lay the foundation of any theoretical system of the social sciences—nay more, that such a discipline as I have in mind would be itself a part, and the most important one, of a general theory of sociology. I think that all this is *compatible* not only with the work of the four men studied by you and with your interpretation of it but also to a great extent with your own system.

I think I have stated frequently and clearly enough in our discussion as well as in my paper my admiration for your work. This does not prevent me from having the insight that you have to go a few steps further in radicalizing your theory in order to arrive at a more general concept which, on the one hand, permits an application to problems actually beyond the reach of your theory and, on the other hand, to a more consistent formulation of your basic ideas, above all of the concept of "subjectivism.'

This is my reply to your general comments and, in my view, this is the most important part of our discussion. As I do not have the intention of bothering you with a discussion which you perhaps do not like at all, I had better stop here for today and wait until I learn from you whether you would be interested after all in hearing what I should have to answer to the many extremely interesting particular questions raised in the rest of your letters. I dare say that I agree with very many of your observations and that there are some where I feel your way of seeing certain problems is the better one. For others, of course, my approach seems to me the more adequate. But I would enter into these special questions only if I could hope that you feel as I do that the whole argument *is* indeed worth the trouble, since your summing up of the whole discussion seems to culminate in some doubt as to this very point. My only aim has been and is to discuss a few of the most important problems of our science with one of the most competent men I have met in this country.

May I finish with an anecdote Richard Wagner relates of Beethoven. An English lord submitted to Beethoven one of his compositions asking him to mark with a cross those passages of his score which Beethoven did not like for one reason or another. Beethoven sent him back his manuscript in a cover over the whole length of which he had carefully painted a cross.

I feel you have quite definitely done the same with my paper. For several reasons, indeed, I am sorry to say, you did not like it at all. Of course it never had been my intention to publish a paper on your work with whose whole basic concept you no less disagree than with all its particulars. My respect for the author and the book is far too great and my polemical temper far too small that I should wish to present to the scientific public an essay on your work which you, unfortunately, consider as inadequate and irrelevant.

Please consider therefore my manuscript as what it was meant from the beginning, a rather lengthy, private letter to the author, whose book I had studied for many months carefully and with great personal advantage.

Sincerely yours,
Alfred Schutz

Parsons: *"Not to become involved in a misunderstanding."* (March 29, 1941)

Dear Dr. Schutz:

Thank you for your long letter. I shall not attempt to answer it in detail now as that would involve a rather extended discussion. I do hope, however, that it will not be necessary for us to become involved in a sort of misunderstanding. I realize, of course, that my critical remarks about various things in your manuscript were rather sharply formulated, but I did not in the least intend them to be derogatory but only to state my own position as clearly as I possibly could. Of course I greatly appreciate the great amount of time and trouble you have put into the study of my work and, though perhaps on an unduly limited basis, I have honestly tried to understand what you were saying; and it is significant, it seems to me, that it is not at all easy in an essay like yours to distinguish between its aspect as a critical discussion of the work of another author and as an exploration of a field of problems. It is true, of course, that I paid primary attention to your discussion in its critical aspect, but that does not seem to me to be incompatible with a sincere desire to further clarify the problems. It seemed to me that at a good many points you did not have an adequate understanding of many of the problems which had been most significant to me in the development of the book, and I did my best to state the issues clearly and explain wherein my own formulation would differ from yours.

To me the most important question would seem to be whether we really have succeeded in joining the issue of a fruitful discussion in this field. Your statement that I don't seem to be as much interested in your problems as you are in mine may quite possibly be correct. If so, this would seem to rest primarily on one of two facts. Either, as I felt when I wrote the letters, the things which you are primarily concerned with discussing are not of the first order of importance for my particular range of theoretical interests or, on the other hand, I have somehow failed to grasp their significance. I do not wish to claim with very great confidence that I have done so. It is true that I have not devoted anywhere nearly as careful a study to your book as you have to mine, but I am not altogether unfamiliar with it. I read it shortly after it appeared some years ago and, while I found much of it interesting, I did not find it of primary significance for the problems I was then working on in that stage of the development of my book. I remember about 1937 having a rather long conversation with Schelting about it and saying essentially that I could not see that for the purposes of my treatment of Max Weber, for instance, it was necessary to go into the kind of analysis of the subjective point of view in relation to the time element which was the central theme of your analysis. I did not feel particularly competent in this field, and I certainly had no reason to be positively critical of your analysis; but I frankly admit it did not arouse an intense interest in the sense in which the work of such men as Weber and Durkheim have done. It is quite possible that I was simply wrong in that judgment, and I fully intend to go back to your book as soon as I have an opportunity—indeed, I should have done so in connection with your manuscript.

At the same time, pending a more mature judgment on this question, I certainly did feel in your manuscript that there were a sufficiently large number of and sufficiently serious questions where it seemed to me that your interpretation of my book was seriously deficient, so that I cannot yet feel that my relative ignorance of your fields of interest is a sufficient explanation of our differences. If you feel that you can supply me with definite evidence of the bearing of your analysis on specific empirical problems, I am very much inclined to think that would be the best bridge between us that we could build. Even with regard to the things you mention toward the end of your letter about the role of the *alter ego* I cannot yet see the difference it would make if these considerations were taken into account with respect, for instance, to such a problem as that of the relations between Protestantism and the modern institutional order.

Perhaps I could say just one word about the now "famous" footnote at the bottom of page 762. I certainly agree that in the treatment of timeless culture systems the categories of action are irrelevant. My statement, however, and so far as I am aware its whole context, was concerned with systems of action as such and not with cultural systems. You may remember that their discussion played an important part in my discussion of Max Weber's methodology in the final section on Action and Complexes of Meaning. The same discussion was brought up again in the final chapter in the distinction between the sciences of action and culture. In that context it would seem that my interpretation was hardly anything but obvious. Pending further reading of your work, I should be inclined to say that when the level is reached where the sciences of action, as you said in your last letter, "deal exclusively with the objects constituted by and through acts of an actor without considering the actor and his acts," that it ceases to be a theory of action, whatever else it may become.

I think perhaps there is not much point in attempting to carry the discussion further until I have had an opportunity to go into your book further. In the meantime, I hope you will believe me when I say that I am thoroughly devoid of any personal feeling about your criticism and wish to keep the question as far as possible on an objective and scientific level.

Sincerely yours,
Talcott Parsons

Schutz: *"Discussion is a poor 'Ersatz' for a dialogue."* (April 21, 1941)

Dear Professor Parsons:

Thank you very much for your kind letter of March 29th, which relieved my anxiety that our "antagonism" in certain scientific questions—if any—had also affected our personal relations as far as your feelings were concerned. I am, therefore, very happy to learn that such is not the case, and this after all is to me the most important point. Your letter gives me hope that this attitude remains as firm on your side as it always has been on mine, and if this is true, further clarification of the issue between us will be possible.

If I referred in my last letter to my own writings, I did so exclusively with the purpose of giving you an explanation of the double goal I had in mind in writing my paper: first, to give a survey of your theory and, secondly, to demonstrate to what extent it is compatible with my own work. But neither am I so pretentious as to think that my book could be put on even approximately the same level as the works of masters like Weber or Durkheim, nor do I think very highly of its appeal to the reader's interest. Maybe it is entirely wrong and insufficient. But although I feel very humble concerning the *solutions* offered by me, I am quite sure that the *problems* treated in the book are *genuine* problems of the social sciences which have to be solved in one way or another. And as the problems and not my solutions are important for our discussion, it is not at all necessary that you bother with my book again if you want to continue our exchange of opinion.

It is really a pity that we are living in such distant places. A discussion by letter is but a poor "Ersatz" for a dialogue in which a misunderstanding can be dissipated immediately, and which at any rate saves time.

For the time being, I am kept quite occupied, as many unexpected things have to be done simultaneously in my vocational and avocational life. But I will try to send you some notes in a few weeks which I had prepared as comments to your previous letters.

With kindest regards,

Sincerely yours,
Alfred Schutz

EDITOR'S NOTE

To my knowledge no further notes or letters were exchanged between Talcott Parsons and Alfred Schutz. Both kept to their decision to keep their dispute a private affair. The two men moved apart into rather distant social worlds.

Professor Parsons is at Harvard University in Cambridge, Massachusetts. Its Department of Social Relations was founded in 1946 to become the institutional frame for his large-scale endeavors toward a General Theory of Action and System Theory. The reader will find the prefaces and introductions to his various books full of biographical details of his life work. In addition, Talcott Parsons has written an autobiographical essay, which has just been published.[1]

Alfred Schutz died in 1959, at the age of sixty. The social theorist for whom scientific thought and everyday life defined two rather distinct and separate realms of experience upheld a similar division in his personal life. His working days in New York City were divided between the daily routine of banking (since graduating from the University of Vienna he had held fulltime positions as legal counsel for various banks) and the scholarly world of social theory and philosophy at the Graduate Faculty of the New School for Social Research in New York. Only in 1953 did Schutz give up this tremendous double load. For a few years thereafter he was free to concentrate full time on his teaching at the New School and his studies of the Structures of the Life World.[2]

112

PART III

Retrospect

Talcott Parsons:
A 1974 Retrospective Perspective[1]

I think it should be remembered that this contact with Dr. Schutz took place more than thirty years ago and, unfortunately, was broken off in the Spring of 1941. I sincerely hope that my own thinking has not ceased to develop in the long intervening period. I am therefore writing now from the point of view of the way I see some of these problems in 1974, not the way I saw them in 1940 or 1941 or in *The Structure of Social Action,* which was put on paper a few years before that. It will in the nature of the case be impossible for me to give a fully detailed commentary on all the significant points which came up. I should rather like to concentrate on two or three main considerations which seem to me to be particularly salient from my present retrospective perspective.

Perhaps I had best start with what is to me the central issue between Dr. Schutz and myself, namely, that of the status of what we have both called "the subjective point of view." The primary difference, it seems to me, is already indicated in his opening statement, where he criticizes the concept of fact which I introduced in *The Structure of Social Action,* leaning in the first instance on a well-known paper of L.J. Henderson, but taking a position which I think in certain fundamentals goes back to Kant. The fundamental point here is that I defined a fact as a *statement about* one or more phenomena of the external world rather than as itself a phenomenon. Schutz takes issue with this and suggests that something like "experience" of phenomena is attainable without the mediation of what Henderson called a conceptual scheme, Kant the categories of the understanding. The problems at issue in this discussion are then applied to what has sometimes been called "the state of mind" of an actor, either an actor as observed by an external scientific observer or an actor reflecting upon his own action.

Though I think I have become considerably more sophisticated in understanding these matters since the early 1940s, I still adhere with undiminished conviction to what from this point of view may be called a Kantian point of view. It seems to me that this connects with the importance of the Kantian influence on Weber's work and that my view is basically in accord with Weber's. This is to say that the rational understanding of human action, including especially the subjective states of minds of actors, requires the combination of the equivalent of what Kant called sense data with categorization, which is to my mind ultimately a cultural entity. It seems to me that Schutz on the other hand takes the view that the subjective state of the actor is accessible to immediate experience through what Husserl called "phenomenological reduction" without the necessity of such "experience" being organized in terms of any kind of a "conceptual scheme," to use Henderson's phrase. If this is correct, as Kant held, about knowledge of objects in the external world, it seems to me it is *mutatis mutandis* correct about the observation of the "motives" of other actors and the self-observation of acting individuals.

At one level I think it can be said that Freud brought consideration of comparable problems to a new focus. It seems to me clear that Freud's position was Kantian–Weberian and not phenomenological. He felt that the understanding of motives required cognitive ordering on the part of not merely the external observer, *vide* the psychoanalyst, but also on the part of the analysand himself in that through interpretation the analysand could come to understand his own motives. This was in my opinion the underlying meaning of Freud's famous aphorism about the psychoanalytic procedure that it could bring about a change such that "where id was there shall ego be."

The "neoKantian" point of view, which I take, is to my mind closely connected with the frame of reference of the theory of action, particularly where social interaction is involved. Now, differently from the phase of the *Structure of Social Action* I conceive a social system as constituted by a plurality of actors who interact with each other. From the point of view of any one actor, both the others and himself as objects constitute the *situation* of action. Every concrete unit in the interaction system, every "individual," is then at the same time *both* an actor, characterized e.g. by "motives" or as Weber said "intentions," *and* an object of the situation of action. I would then treat both actors and objects outside the boundaries of the system of reference as belonging to the environment of that system. This distinction is of paramount importance. Of course within limits the definition of a system for analysis rests on more or less free or even "arbitrary" decisions of the investigator.

The actor-situation, or actor-object distinction of course constitutes a generalization from Descartes' famous dichotomy of knowing subject and object known. In its generalization as a frame of reference for the analysis of action, of course, it ceases to be purely or even predominantly cognitive in reference and includes a variety of components not appropriate to what is only a "theory of knowledge" in the epistemological sense, such as goals, sentiments, norms values, and various others.

I do not accord priority to either the object component of this relational conception or the knowing subject or actor component. In extreme cases there has been the advocacy of the virtually total elimination of one of them in favor of the other. There has also been advocacy of the position that the distinction in itself is totally irrelevant. For example, it has been claimed that there are languages in which the grammatical distinction between subject and predicates does not figure at all—I happen not to believe this allegation. The phenomenological point of view, particularly in the version represented by Schutz, seems to me a relatively modest attempt to give special advantages to the subjective part of the type or if one will one horn of the Cartesian and post-Cartesian dilemma. In doing so, however, as I have suggested, it seems to me to have leaned too far in the direction of attributing a quasimetaphysical status to immediate knowledge of the subjective and a corresponding derogation of the importance and certain special roles of objectification.

It is altogether natural that this problem should have become acute with the development of technical theoretical schemes in the field of human action and especially social interaction at the human level. The situations which make this an acute problem became particularly saliently evident in the work of the generation of writers who were the subject of my *The Structure of Social Action.* In one context Durkheim posed the problems most saliently in that he tended to think of the individual actor as acting in a social environment which in its empirical aspect consisted of social facts. Unlike the natural environment of human action, however, the objects in relation to which an actor acted were historically considered "constructed" outcomes of previous human action. They were not in the usual sense natural phenomena. From one point of view they were objects the genesis of which had been determined by the subjective activity of actors. In some sense or other they were both objective and subjective in meaning at the same time.

It seems to me essential always to keep clearly in mind that the same concrete entities dealt with by a theory of action are both subjectively oriented actors and objects. This duality of status applies not only to discrete types of unit or entity, but is an analytical line which must be drawn through every concrete entity of this class. One implication of this is amply documented in the history of thought, namely, that the self becomes object to the thinking person as formulated, for example, in Mead's distinction between the Me and the I. Certain implications of this, however, must be carried farther.

I may next come to a topic on which I remember having had rather extended, but not terribly productive, discussions with Dr. Schutz, and with respect to which subsequent intellectual developments which have impinged on me have introduced what seems to me to be a very considerable clarification. I think I would formulate these problems somewhat differently from the way Dr. Schutz did, but I think I understand very much better than I did about 1940 what is at issue.

This concerns the question of time orientations. They are not very prominent in the material you have edited, but certainly are very important in the background. As I remember, Schutz was particularly insistent on the fundamental distinction between the meaning of time orientation prospectively, that is, from the point of view of an actor, in initiating and carrying out what Schutz calls a "project" of action, and secondly, the meaning of time perspective in a retrospective situation where an actor and, indeed, also an observer is conceived as thinking about what has in fact occurred, including his own agency in bringing it about, and "explaining" these occurrences.

There may be various other differences, but I have become increasingly aware of one which seems to me altogether fundamental. Part of my perspective rests on my very long-standing conviction that all scientific analysis is at some level and to some degree abstract. This is a point of view I derived particularly from Max Weber and from A.N. Whitehead. The position of a human actor clearly involves limitations which necessitate such abstraction in his viewing of the situation in which he acts and particularly in the perspective of future conditions and events, including the consequences of his own intervention, which he must take into account in conceiving a project in Schutz's sense, and proceeding to implement his plan for it. I have found it convenient to refer to the limitations on possible full determination of the future as focusing in contingencies which may arise in the course of implementation of a project, but which cannot be predicted in detail in advance.

After a course of action has been completed, however, the situation is very different and a substantially higher order of determinateness becomes feasible. The basic reason for this is that at the many junctures along the way where there may have been contingently open alternatives when seen prospectively, something specific actually has occurred, and this something specific constitutes a selection among the alternatives which were previously open. Therefore, the attempt to explain how an outcome of an action process came about, whether this is done by the actor himself or some observer, can be much more determinate than can the prospective view. This, obviously, is because action, like other empirical processes, is in many fundamental respects irreversible. What has happened has, in fact, happened, and its consequences will have to be coped with.

At the time that Schutz and I were discussing these problems what is now frequently called the cybernetic point of view was scarcely on the horizon. This seems to me, however, to have served immensely to clarify this kind of consideration, essentially by introducing a component of what one might call limited reversibility. The obvious point is that when the actor encounters an unexpected contingency, he may take action which he perceives not to be in accord with his plan for his project. Negative feedback about the course the action is taking and forecasting of the probable consequences can lead him to reconsider and to take a different tack, that is, to take corrective action. It is therefore possible through retreating a short part of the way to reorient the course of action and bring the probabilities into closer accord with realization of the goal which has been fixed in the project.

It seems to me that looking at action from this point of view has a very important bearing on the problem of rationality. An older perspective often seemed to require the postulate that an action could be rational seen prospectively only if every single step in it could be accurately foreseen and decided upon at the beginning of the course of action. The cybernetic mode of coping with the unexpected contingencies, however, makes that postulate unnecessary or greatly restricts the scope which must be assumed. Indeed, it seems to me substantially to broaden the scope of the concept of rational action. One condition remains, namely, that the goal of action should not be "utopian" in the sense that it is impossible of attainment given the exigencies of the situation, including the capacities of actors. This implies that there is a sufficiently accurate estimate of the range and limits of contingencies so that the actor is not in a position of postulating too many impossibilities. Action, however, to be rational, need not have a built-in guarantee of success. The factor of contingency which I have been stressing may include the possibility and varying degrees of probability that things might happen which would make attainment of the goal impossible, though there would be sufficient probability that this would not be the case so that the investment in attempting to attain the goal could not be treated as irrational. This would be, of course, an element of risk with which we are quite familiar.

Considerations of this sort are particularly important when the type of action to which criteria of rationality are being applied involved social interaction. This is because, from the point of view of any given actor of reference, a major source of contingency is uncertainty about how his interaction partners will "react" to his actions. It seems to me that as early as the work I and my colleagues did on *Toward a General Theory of Action* and *The Social System,* I had advanced considerably beyond the level I had attained in the discussions with Schutz in appreciating the nature of social interaction. This, I think, has a bearing on certain of the problems still to be discussed. I should also point out, before going on, that the above discussion of rationality applies above all to what Weber called *Zweckrationalität.* The same order of criteria of success and feasibility are much more difficult to apply; at least they would have to be differently applied in Weber's other case of *Wertra-tionalität.*

A third and particularly important consideration is not covered by Dr. Schutz in his article on my work and of which I was not clearly aware at the time of writing *The Structure of Social Action:* the implication of what has generally come to be called the internalization of objects in the life history of the human individual. Weber clearly had a somewhat undeveloped version of this idea. But it was particularly developed by Freud on the one hand, Durkheim on the other, and by the group of American social psychologists who have come to be called "social interactionists," notably, Mead, Thomas, and Cooley. It seems to me that the phenomenon of internalization renders very strong support to my point of view because objects not only in the Cartesian sense, but also that of Freud, and cultural norms, especially as emphasized by Durkheim, are not devoid of categorical components. They do not constitute pure and unadulterated "experience."

This set of considerations seems to me to make the rigidity of the dichotomy Schutz draws, specifically with reference to time, untenable except at the most abstract analytical levels. This is incorporated in his distinction between "in-order-to" motives and "because" motives and the sharp distinction between the subjective experience in the course of carrying out an action project on the one hand and reflection on what has happened after the completion of the program on the other. The implication I have in mind is that action processes themselves are in important parts the outcome of the existence of objects, not merely the conditionally and instrumentally significant objects of the actor's situation, but also the objects internalized as part of his own personality or self. Freud in his later years went very far in this direction, not confining internalization to the superego parts of the personality, but extending it quite explicitly to the ego and inferentially to the id. If so prominent a part of the personality of the human individual as the ego is, to use Freud's phrase, "the precipitate of lost objects," it can hardly be true that his subjective experience is analytically totally independent of the object world. To be sure the relevant category of objects is not "natural objects," but what I and others have called "social objects," a phrasing which is meant to accentuate the fact that they are or have been actors in the present technical sense.

It seems to me that failure to deal with the problem of internalization is an example of a tendency which is prominent in Schutz's writings, very much including the paper and correspondence now under discussion, to pose unduly sharp either/or alternatives. The deepest underlying one seems to be the alternative between object status and subject status for any given entity of reference. The combinatorial aspects of actors thus seems to me to appear at many different levels. One of these is the experience of actors in the course of action. They act as well as think, in my opinion, in "terms of a conceptual scheme" to use the phrase I borrowed from L.J. Henderson's definition of fact. They also appraise or evaluate in terms of a conceptual scheme in the retrospective understanding of their own and others' action. In principle the situation is not different for the scientific observer whose treatment of the subjective point of view must also in my opinion take place in terms of a conceptual scheme, that is, some set of categories in the Kantian sense.

It seems to me that Dr. Schutz poses an altogether unrealistically sharp contrast between the point of view of the actor and the point of view of the scientific observer and analyst, virtually dissociating them from each other. Quite the contrary it seems to me that they are closely connected and that "doing" science is an extreme type of action.

This seems to me to be involved in what for long was to me a puzzling contention of the phenomenological school which is prominent in Schutz's work and has been carried on by such followers of him as Harold Garfinkel. This is the special emphasis on phenomenological access to what is called "everyday life" and the insistence that everyday life in this sense is radically distinct from any perspective of the scientific observer. This, of course, constitutes a problem which is central to the consideration of rationality. It seems to me to be an unreal dichotomy. There is not a radical break between everyday life and the behavior of scientifically trained people, but science constitutes an accentuation and special clarification of certain components which are present in all human action no matter how untutored the actor may be. Here it seems to me that the perspective of Malinowski in *Magic, Science, and Religion* is extremely instructive. To him "primitive man" acted quite rationally in certain contexts and the paradigms of rational action of a sort which Pareto worked with are quite applicable to, for example, his technology in the field of gardening.

The above considerations are very far from being exhaustive of the problems which have been revived for me and in many cases newly defined by my re-reading of Dr. Schutz's manuscript and the interchanges of correspondence between him and myself. I think, however, that I have covered enough of the centrally important points in this interpretive statement to give a flavor of the way I look at the problems raised in those documents of more than thirty years ago. I hope I am in a position now to give considerably more sophisticated answers than I did in *The Structure of Social Action* or in my conversations and correspondence with Alfred Schutz at the time when it took place.

Richard Grathoff: *How Long a Schutz-Parsons Divide?*

Talcott Parsons' retrospective account is an invitation to continue the debate. Alfred Schutz cannot reply. But scholarly discourse by necessity is an open round and the reader, who has followed this far, may wish to pursue the issues on his or her own. This final editorial note focuses attention on two points. First, there is, of course, the perennial problem of all translations: on the one hand, transferring the Weberian terminology of social action from its original German into the English context and on the other hand the discourse enters the uneven semantic terrain of German and English concept formations which both scholars grasped differently. Second, one might recall briefly the four major issues of this correspondence: The *Weberian Suggestion,* which is especially effected by semantic differences of the debate; the *Kantian Problem* as well as the *Cartesian Dilemma,* both of which found explicit mention in the Parsons' retrospect; finally, the *Schutz–Parsons Divide,* which draws attention to the question of the legitimacy of a sociology of everyday life.

Charles S. Peirce has coined the imaginative notion of "the purport of a word," the load of traditional and historical meanings a word carries along enriching itself in each of its usages and contexts, leaving in turn a trace of itself when spoken of.[2] Broad terms, like "experience" and "action," carry an especially wide purport plastering the debate with semantic ambiguities that can only be mitigated in the long run by some conceptual consensus. In the 1940s sociological inquiry into this field of social action had just begun. The conceptual dispute, for instance, about the "correct" Weber interpretation among American sociologists could hardly be anticipated.[3] Hence, a look at the purport of "action" and of "experience" in both languages suggests itself.

The term "experience" hides an ambiguity which becomes apparent in its twin German equivalents of *Erlebnis* and *Erfahrung*. While the former means an experience in the immediate fullness of a lived-through experiencing, say, between persons face to face, the latter distinguishes experience as something to be reflected upon. While the first is always immediate, the latter, for instance, can be distinguished (in a bit of phenomenological terminology) with respect to "predicative" and "pre-predicative" experiences. For Schutz, this difference is of utmost significance. Preserving it leads the translator into cumbersome constructions opening up problem areas which Schutz later dealt with in great detail in some of his most important methodological essays.[4]

This ambiguity, I contend, justifies further careful analysis. Support comes from another linguistic quarter, namely, from a critique of the current reception of Pareto. In a recent careful exposition of Pareto's work, Piet Tommissen has discussed the difficulty of rendering the Italian *sperimento* into German and English respectively, since it carries the double meaning of "experiment" and "experience."[5] Of course, historical linguists have shown that earlier English usage did not distinguish between the two terms either. Tommissen criticizes Joseph Schumpeter for favoring the first connotation. Thus Pareto's "*economica sperimentale*" turns into an "experimental economics," a shift in meaning, which favors the later trend toward system-oriented concept formations. We can go no further here than to mention the possible implications for Talcott Parsons' Pareto interpretations which are marginal to the present discussion.

Of immediate concern is the translation of the terms "act" and "action." Their German equivalents of *Handlung* (act) and *Handeln* (action) are reminiscent of trade and barter, of commercial traffic as well as deals of a more shady kind; even the store which sells goods and groceries may be meant by the term *Handlung*. The purport of this word carries distinct economic references. More important, however, is the additional stress the Weberian methodology itself lays in supporting this origin: Weber's original studies all start from the socio-political structure of economic organizations; his dissertation, for instance, analyzes the highly informal trading companies of the middle ages and their successive rationalization.[6] These studies have permanently coined his concept formation.

The Weberian notion of action as projected, problem-solving, and economy-directed behavior comes up against a different semantic context in the English. In English the terms "action" and "act" refer more often to the realm of law, to legal contexts, say, to an "act of Congress," to the institutional traffic between offices, bureaus, and the like. This purport of the English term brings Parsons' usage, for instance, of his "unit act" into a much closer relationship, say, to George Herbert Mead's conceptions in his "Philosophy of the Act" than their theoretical differences would otherwise suppose.

Such semantic finesse must be relied upon at least on two occasions: first, when considering concrete empirical problems and actual translations; second, where the epistemic claim of a discipline turns toward a problem area previously staked out under already established paradigms and suddenly opened up by a different perspective. This is, of course, what Schutz insists upon. The major issues of the Schutz/Parsons debate illuminate this epistemic claim of sociology to the world of everyday life.[7] Schutz had this claim in mind when he insisted that Parsons needed only "to go a few steps further in radicalizing" his theory.

While the *Weberian Suggestion* directed methodological interest in the foundation of the social sciences toward the texture of social action, Talcott Parsons and Alfred Schutz pursued this suggestion in different directions.[8] Today this proposal has to meet another challenge, as pointed out by Talcott Parsons in his retrospect: The emergence of cybernetics and the subsequent system-analyses of social action. These, of course, developed after Schutz and Parsons debated the question of rationality in and subsequent to the Harvard Seminar on Rationality. It has been the achievement of another immigrant group, namely, Johann von Neumann and his colleagues in Princeton, who succeeded in developing the exact, i.e., the mathematical analysis of strategic action patterns.[9] Without the tools of mathematical game theory neither cybernetics nor a modern system theory could have gotten far. But now, the calculation of strategic action patterns, the formalization of the norms and rationalities of economic market behaviors, of political action patterns and the like seemed to become just a numerical problem.

Nevertheless, the *Kantian Problem* returns now in full force to the foreground of methodological debate. The Kantian position obviously had to gain an enormous impetus at that very moment when one succeeded in formalizing and mathematizing some core systems of action which seemed to allow an access to a crucial problem of everyday life: the study of social change as an evolution of social structures. The Kantian imagery that one should be able to subsume common-sense patterns of norms and normalities as if they were like some regularities of nature suddenly found new support when such rules reached the level of mathematical representations.[10] There is nothing surprising in this development, if one only reconsiders the Darwinian vision: to grasp systematically the structures of evolution in natural life.

But what are the limits of any such theory construction of social action? Let us recall the two positions presented in this little volume. Schutz draws his line with this remark: "The theory of social action ... stands or falls with the results of an analysis of the relation between the subjective point of view and the terms which sociologists actually use in performing their concrete research work."[11] Clearly, the possibility of formulating a theory of social action remains for Schutz an open one. The *Cartesian Dilemma,* i.e., the problem of intersubjectivity, is still the stumbling block on the way toward a solution.[12] For Talcott Parsons, this problem does not arise at all: He defines the concrete other as an environmental problem. There is perhaps no clearer phrase to show their differences than his terse retrospective statement: "Doing science is an extreme type of action."[13] For him science comes close to being a theory of action itself. For Schutz, science and everyday life remain distinct and separate realms of meaning, experience, and action.

How serious is this *Schutz-Parsons Divide?* One may recall that Schutz and Parsons share at least a common base line. Both insist that every study of social action must begin with the individual actor himself. While Parsons takes account of the individual actor in terms of situational references within action systems, Schutz insists that a grasp of the concrete actor and his performances, of his interests and motives should become accessible through the study of the structure of relevances in everyday life.[14]

Can this divide be overcome? A host of questions remain, which cannot simply be answered by a courageous adherence to extreme positions. Shall we take rationality just as a feature of the evolutionary process, as schemes of some implicit logicality, which are emerging successively in the form of social structures in everyday life? Or shall we take rationality and the order in everyday life as a successive rationalization of a common-sense world, as a spreading evolution of systems and systematized structures? Or should we insist that the rationality of the sciences is a unique, but nevertheless historical product, perhaps even an historical accident, illuminating the specious and multitudinous worlds of everyday life, but neither an integral nor a permanent part of them?

At the time of the debate Schutz was deeply concerned about these issues. The experiences of an immigrant, the suffering of the destruction of a social and cultural world as if it were a historical whim of the moment, the knowledge of a barbarian potential of mankind to eliminate itself: these experiences left Schutz in no mood to assent to the idea that humane norms and values were just teleological implications of some evolutionary progress. For him, Parsons' references toward the consensual and voluntaristic moments of social action remained all too ambiguous. Though Schutz seems to move closer to Talcott Parsons' position here, he starts from a different terrain. The structure of social action, for Schutz, is a social construction of reality, a purposefully intersubjective process, in which the pre-givenness of an historical and cultural world is ongoingly rebuilt.[15] But to what avail? In a letter to his friend Aron Gurwitsch, just a few days after his final note to Talcott Parsons, Schutz wrote:

> You are still optimist enough to believe that phenomenology may save itself among the ruins of this world—as the *philosophica aera perennis?* I do not believe so. More likely the African natives must prepare themselves for the ideas of national socialism. This shall not prevent us from dying the way we have lived; and we must try, therefore, to build that order into *our* world, which we must find lacking in—our *world.* The whole conflict is hidden in this shift of emphasis.[16]

NOTES

Introduction

1. Max Weber, "The Fundamental Concepts of Sociology," in *The Theory of Social and Economic Organisation,* first translated from the German *Wirtschaft und Gesellschaft* by A. M. Henderson and Talcott Parsons (New York: Oxford University Press, 1947). In a new translation of this Weberian opus, *Economy and Society* by Günter Roth and Claus Wittich (New York: Badminster Press, 1968), see Roth's introduction for a discussion of Talcott Parsons' interpretation of Max Weber. Alfred Schutz, "Some Basic Problems of Interpretive Sociology," in *The Phenomenology of the Social World,* trans. George Walsh and Frederick Lehnert (Evanston, Ill.: Northwestern University Press, 1967). Originally published as *Der sinnhafte Aufbau der sozialen Welt* (Vienna: Springer, 1932;· Frankfurt: Suhrkamp, 1974). Talcott Parsons, "The Theory of Social Action," in *The Structure of Social Action* (New York: McGraw-Hill, 1937).

2. Helmuth Plessner, "Der cartesianische Einwand," in *Die Stufen des Organischen und der Mensch* (Berlin: De Gruyter, 1928). Charles S. Peirce, "The Spirit of Cartesianism," in *Collected Papers,* vol. 5, par. 264–65 (Cambridge: Harvard University Press, 1934–58). See a summary review in Richard Grathoff, "Mind and Nature: The Consequences of Cartesian Dualism for the Social Sciences," in *Contemporary European Sociology,* ed. Tom Burns (London: Penguin, forthcoming).

3. The most radical attempt (not restricted to social science, but to objectivating sciences as such) is Edmund Husserl's *Cartesian Meditations,* trans. Dorion Cairns (The Hague: Nijhoff, 1960). First French publication in 1931. For a summary of the problem and a sketch of his own position, see Alfred Schutz, "The Problem of Transcendental Intersubjectivity in Husserl," in *Collected Papers,* vol. 3 (The Hague: Nijhoff, 1966).

4. See p. 115, this volume.

5. Immanuel Kant, *Kritik der reinen Vernunft*, 1781, A 141: "This schematism of our understanding is a hidden art deep in the human soul, the true workings of which we hardly ever shall wrestle from nature to present it openly to the inquiring eye" (my trans.).

6. Maurice Merleau-Ponty, "Other People and the Human World," in *Phenomenology of Perception* (London: Routledge and Kegan Paul, 1962). See also his other writings. For a careful synopsis of this problem, see Richard M. Zaner, *The Problem of Embodiment* (The Hague: Nijhoff, 1964). In addition see the works of Emmanuel Levinas.

7. For reviews of Schutz's book in the 1930s, see "A New Approach to the Methodology of the Social Sciences," Alfred Stonier and Karl Bode, *Economica*, vol. 4, 1937, 406–423; Franz Borkenau, *Zeitschrift für Sozialforschung*, 1932; J. Gerhardt, *Jahrbücher für Nationalökonomie*, 140, 1934, Heft 5; Paul Plaut, *Zeitschrift für angewandte Psychologie*, 44, Heft 5–6; Erich Voegelin in *Zeitschrift für öffentliches Recht*, 14, 1934, 668–72; Felix Kaufmann, *Deutsche Literaturzeitung*, 36, 1932, 1712–16. For reviews of Parsons' book at the time, see W. R. Crawford, *Annals of the American Academy of Political and Social Sciences*, 1938, 198, 178–79; F. N. House, *American Journal of Sociology*, 1939, 45, 129–30; C. Kirkpatrick, *Journal of Political Economics*, 1938, 46, 588–89; L. Wirth, *American Sociological Review*, 1939, 4, 399–404.

8. March 29, 1941. Parsons knew Alexander von Schelting from Heidelberg. His single and important book, *Max Webers Wissenschaftslehre: Das logische Problem der historischen Kulturerkenntnis; die Grenzen der Soziologie des Wissens* (Tübingen: Mohr, 1934), contains two short "Exkurse" on the problem of rationality (pp. 12–18) significant for the later discourse in the Harvard Seminar on Rationality.

9. *Coll. Pap.* 1, pp. 138, n21. For the working paper see the German edition of Alfred Schutz, *Gesammelte Aufsätze*, vol. 1, (The Hague: Nijhoff, 1971), pp. 136–39. The above quote (my trans.) is on p. 139.

10. Published under the title "The Problem of Rationality in the Social World" in *Economica*, vol. 10, May 1943, pp. 130–49, and in *Collected Papers*, vol. 2, pp. 64–90. Arvid Broderson's editorial remark in the *Collected Papers* contains a minor mistake that

this paper was "presented at the Interdepartmental Conference at Harvard University 1942" (p. xiii).

11. Schutz referred incidentally to this paper in his letter of Nov. 15, 1940 ("as far as your manuscript on rationality is concerned"), and Parsons mentioned it earlier in a short letter of Jan. 24, 1940, to Schutz not included in this volume: "My little discussion of rationality." A copy of this Parsons manuscript is among the Schutz papers.

12. Unpublished parts of the manuscript of Schutz's Harvard lecture (for published parts, see note 10). Mrs. Schutz recently gave her consent to microfilm all scholarly papers and correspondence, complete copies of which have been deposited at the Sozialwissenschaftliches Archiv, Universität Konstanz, and at the Centre for Advanced Phenomenological Research, Waterloo, Ontario. Quoting from these sources: film 1, pp. 119–77, esp. pp. 2–3. The original papers of Alfred Schutz are to be deposited in the Beinecke Library of Yale University.

13. The following two letters refer to two different Parsons manuscripts on rationality. For the first ms. see note 11. As for the "second, larger manuscript," the editor of the German edition of this correspondence, Walter Sprondel, has identified it on the basis of his research into the Schutzean notes on Parsons: its title is "Actor, Situation, and Normative Patterns. An Essay in the Theory of Social Action" (Schutz papers, film 1, 561–66). Sprondel suggests it may be an earlier version of the Parsons–Shils essay, "Values, Motives, and Systems of Action" (in *Toward a General Theory of Action,* Harvard University Press, 1951). The letters mention Emanuel Winternitz, who taught from 1938 to 1941 at the Fogg Museum in Harvard, and Eric Voegelin, then teaching at the University of Alabama. Both had been close friends of Alfred Schutz since their Vienna times. Richard H. Williams taught at the University of Buffalo; he translated the first Schutzean essays into English. See *Coll. Pap.* 1, 118, author's note.

Part I: Inquiry into the Structure of Social Action

1. Talcott Parsons, *The Structure of Social Action.* Hereafter cited as *SofSA.*

2. *SofSA,* 698.

3. *SofSA*, 41 (italics from Schutz). See L. J. Henderson, *An Approximate Definition of Fact* (University of California Studies in Philosophy, 1932).—*Ed.*

4. *SofSA*, 719ff.

5. *SofSA*, 43.

6. *SofSA*, 731 and 739.

7. *SofSA*, 757f.

8. *SofSA*, 734f.

9. *SofSA*, 756.

10. *SofSA*, 725.

11. *SofSA*, 44.

12. *SofSA*, 44.

13. *SofSA*, 75 (Schutz's italics.—*Ed.*)

14. *SofSA*, 77.

15. *SofSA*, 733 and 45, respectively, for the above quotes.

16. The problem of the time element in action will not be developed in this study. See G. H. Mead, *The Philosophy of the Act* (Chicago: University of Chicago Press, 1938), and *The Philosophy of the Present* (La Salle: Open Court, 1932). I have developed my own point of view in extended analyses in my book *Der sinnhafte Aufbau der sozialen Welt.*

17. *SofSA*, 45f. For the following quotes see p. 47.

18. *SofSA*, 82.

19. *SofSA*, 733.

20. *SofSA*, 634 and 738 for the following quotes.

21. *SofSA*, 52.

22. *SofSA*, 58 (italics mine). For our critical examination of Parsons' theory the role attributed to *scientific* knowledge within the frame of reference of the unit act will be of the greatest importance. Obviously Parsons is influenced by Pareto's theory of logical and non-logical actions. Pareto, too, defined logical actions as "those operations which are logically united to their end, *not only from the point of view of the subject who performs the operations, but also for those who have a more extended knowledge.*" Vilfredo Pareto, *The Mind and Society,* vol. 1 (New York: Harcourt, 1935), § 150.

23. *SofSA*, 64.

24. *SofSA*, 69 and 448.

25. *SofSA*, 453. See Alfred Marshall, *Principles of Economics,* 8th ed. (London: Macmillan, 1925), p. 781.

26. *SofSA*, 457–59.

27. *Sof SA*, 461.

28. *Sof SA*, 467. Parsons calls Durkheim's thesis that society is a reality *sui generis* the "sociologistic theorem" (*Sof SA*, 248).

29. *Sof SA*, 683.

30. *Sof SA*, 717, for the following passage: 718–19.

31. *Sof SA*, 81. Such "non-subjective terms" are for Parsons "environment," "heredity," etc. See *Sof SA*, 82f.

32. *Sof SA*, 81–82, also 79.

33. *Sof SA*, 743–48.

34. *Sof SA*, 741.

35. *Sof SA*, 35n.

36. *Sof SA*, 48–49.

37. *Sof SA*, 732.

38. *Sof SA*, 739–40.

39. *Sof SA*, 748. The *Oxford University Dictionary* explains this bit of Parsonean terminology: *Warp* refers to the "threads which are extended lengthwise in the loom, usually twisted harder than the weft or *woof*, with which these threads are crossed to from the web or piece."—*Ed.*

40. *Sof SA*, 750.

41. *Sof SA*, 762. Schutz refers here to Parsons' footnote on p. 762, which became one focus of the following exchange.—*Ed.*

42. *Sof SA*, 760–62.

43. *Sof SA*, 764.

44. *Sof SA*, 770.

45. *Sof SA*, 768.

46. "On the Theory of Wholes and Parts" and "The Distinction Between Independent and Non-Independent Meanings and the Idea of Pure Grammar," in Edmund Husserl, *Logical Investigations*, vol. 2, trans. J. N. Findlay (London: Routledge and Kegan Paul; New York: The Humanities Press, 1970).

47. It is important that for Pareto, too, "logical" is nothing other than scientifically correct knowledge of facts and relations, the term "scientific" always being understood in the sense of empirically verified knowledge.

48. William James, *Principles of Psychology*, vol. 2 (New York: Holt, 1890), p. 330.

49. For Schutz's distinction between "rational" and "reasonable," see "The Problem of Rationality in the Social World," *Coll. Pap.* 2, p. 74.—*Ed.*

50. For references and a later explication of this theme, see

Alfred Schutz, "Common Sense and Scientific Interpretation of Human Action," *Coll. Pap.* 1, pp. 3–47.—*Ed.*

51. Many experiences in daily life could be cited as proof of this statement. The businessman is not interested in the verifiability by economic theory of his decisions, provided he is given a reasonable chance of profit. The patient is not interested primarily in the scientifically correct treatment ordered by the physician, provided the treatment gives him a chance of health. There is a structural difference not only in the level of concreteness and abstractness, on which theoretical and practical attitudes work, but also and above all in the system of relevances and interests, which necessarily differ for the actor interested only in truth.

52. Here, precisely, lies the great importance of the time element in the theory of action.

53. *Sof SA,* 26.—*Ed.*

54. *Sof SA,* 635. "Motivationsverstehen," in Max Weber, *Wirtschaft und Gesellschaft* (Tübingen: Mohr, 1956), Chap. 1: Soziologische Grundbegriffe, Sec. 1.5. (English: in Parsons' translation, pp. 94–95: "to understand in terms of motive"—*Ed.*)

55. *Der sinnhafte Aufbau der sozialen Welt.* I have borrowed some English terms from the excellent study that A. Stonier and Karl Bode published about my theory. (See footnote 7 of Introduction.—*Ed.*)

56. More detailed in Schutz's later essay "Choosing among Projects of Action," *Coll. Pap.* 1, pp. 67–96. Schutz alludes to his theory of relevances (as "great subjective systems"), published posthumously by R. Zaner, *Reflections on the Problem of Relevance* (New Haven: Yale University Press, 1970).—*Ed.*

57. Schutz often referred in this matter to the following authors: W. I. Thomas, *Social Behavior and Personality* (New York: Social Science Research Council, 1951); Charles H. Cooley, *Social Organization* (New York: Scribners', 1909) and *Human Nature and the Social Order* (New York: Scribners', 1922); George H. Mead, *Mind, Self and Society* (Chicago: University of Chicago Press, 1934); and Gordon Allport, *Personality* (New York: H. Holt, 1937).—*Ed.*

58. Znaniecki, for instance, states that all social phenomena can be described under one of four schemes of reference: 1. Social Personality, 2. Social Act, 3. Social Group, 4. Social Relations. I heartily agree with him, as does Parsons. The deeper reason for

their applicability (at least the first two schemes—the subjective ones) lies in the fact that from the subjective point of view all social phenomena can be broken down into acts of persons within the social world, and in the fact that these acts themselves can be interpreted either as systems of because motives, which form their bases, or as systems of in-order-to motives, which integrate their goals. The first way constitutes the scheme of reference of social personality, the second that of social act. See Florian Znaniecki, *The Method of Sociology* (New York: Farrar and Rinehart, 1934), esp. pp. 107–120.—*Ed.*

59. Under this hypothesis it would be a great problem to show why—speaking always from the subjective point of view—such ultimate values are temporarily admitted, temporarily rejected by the actor.

60. *Sof SA*, 43f., 731, 737.—*Ed.*

61. This does not mean that the social sciences and especially sociology would not be interested in this topic and could leave the whole problem of relevance to philosophers and psychologists for further research. On the contrary, the explanation of the emergence of consistent systems of in-order-to and because motives within the social world is one of the most urgent tasks for the social sciences and especially for a general sociology worthy of the name.

62. *Essai sur les données immédiates de la conscience* (Paris: T. Alcan, 1888). English trans. by T. L. Pogson, *Time and Free Will* (New York: Macmillan, 1910).—*Ed.*

63. Harvey Pinney reproaches Parsons in his fine study "The Theory of Social Action" (*Ethics*, January 1940, 184–92) with the fact that the concept "actor," except for its inclusion among the elements of the unit act, disappears from the other analyses in Parsons book and that therefore Parsons' "theory of act" deals with an "action without an actor." I cannot see that this reproach is justified. The actor, as conceived by Parsons, is an analytical element and therefore an abstraction performed by the scientific observer of the social world. As such he continues to reappear in the further analyses, if not under the name of an actor, then under the name of an ideal-type, constructed by the observer. Because Parsons accepted the tenet of Znaniecki that every social phenomenon can be described (among other categories) under the frame of reference either of action or of personality, he did not need to go farther into an analysis of the actor within a study

restricting itself to action analysis. On the other hand, it must be regretted that Parsons' concept of the unit act uncritically merges subjective and objective elements—a great shortcoming of the logical uniformity of his theories.

64. From here on, this essay is mainly a statement of Schutz's own theory. It has been previously published under the title "The Social World and the Theory of Social Action," in *Coll. Pap.* 2, pp. 3–19.—*Ed.*

65. Schutz refers later (*Coll. Pap.* 1, p. 168) in this context to Bertrand Russell, *Our Knowledge of the External World* (London, 1922), Lecture 3, pp. 72ff., and to Rudolf Carnap, *Scheinprobleme der Philosophie* (Berlin, 1928)—*Ed.*

66. John B. Watson, *Psychology from the Standpoint of a Behaviorist,* 3rd ed. (Philadelphia: Lippincott, 1929), pp. 38f.

67. The foregoing remarks are only partially true for the so-called behavioristic position of the great philosopher and sociologist G. H. Mead. See *Mind, Self and Society* (Chicago: University of Chicago Press, 1934), esp. pp. 2ff. An analysis of Mead's most important theory must be reserved for another occasion. [Schutz did not write such a study. But see, for instance, Maurice Natanson, *The Social Dynamics of George H. Mead* (Washington: 1956; The Hague: Nijhoff, 1973).—*Ed.*]

68. This is the main point of departure for the work of Maurice Merleau-Ponty. See his *The Structure of Behavior* (Boston: Beacon, 1963) for the critique of the behaviorist's position, and his *Phenomenology of Perception* (New York: Routledge, 1962).—*Ed.*

69. To be as precise as possible: on the level of what we have just called "objective schemes" the dichotomy of subjective and objective points of view does not even become visible. It emerges only with the basic assumption that the social world *may* be referred to activities of individual human beings and to the meaning those individuals bestow on their social life-world. But it is precisely this basic assumption, which alone makes the problem of subjectivity in the social sciences accessible, that holds for modern sociology in general, and especially for Parsons and the four men whose works he discussed.

70. A later version of this "basic postulate of the methodology of social science" indicates an interesting development in Schutz's thought, namely, "that the conduct of man has to be explained *as if* occurring among problematic possibilities." *Coll. Pap.* 1, p. 83.—*Ed.*

71. The term "thing," used in both cases in its broadest sense, covers not only corporal objects but also "ideal" or mental ones. [For the various connotations of "understanding," see *Phenomenology of the Social World*, 21.—*Ed.*]

72. Of course the interpretation of natural things as products of the agency of another intelligence (though not a human one) is always an overt possibility. The life of the tree is then the result of the activities of a demon or of a dryad, etc.

73. An attempt was made by the present writer in his book: *Der sinnhafte Aufbau der sozialen Welt.* [See also his later essay "Choosing among Projects of Action," in *Coll. Pap.* 1, pp. 67–96. —*Ed.*]

74. "Soziales Handeln ...welches seinem von dem oder den Handelnden gemeinten Sinn nach auf das Verhalten *anderer* bezogen wird und daran in seinem Ablauf orientiert ist." Max Weber, *Wirtschaft und Gesellschaft*, p. 1; and Parsons, *SofSA*, p. 641. (See Parsons' translation, p. 88, last line.—*Ed.*)

75. Parsons did not study in his *Structure of Social Action* the modifications that his basic concept of the unit act necessarily undergoes if applied to social interrelationships, i.e., to social acts mutually oriented to one another. Quite rightly he rejects atomistic methods in the social sciences. But, on the other hand, he has not overcome the most dangerous form of atomism, namely, that of building up a system of social action by isolated acts of isolated individuals without entering further into the problem of social acts and society as such.

76. Compare with Schutz's later statement on "The Scientific Model of the Social World," *Coll. Pap.* 1, pp. 40–44.—*Ed.*

77. I have sketched some of the principles ruling the formation of ideal types in a lecture delivered in the Faculty Club of Harvard University under the title "The Problem of Rationality in the Social World." (Later published in *Coll. Pap.* 2, pp. 64–88; this lecture of April 1940 initiated the present discourse between Schutz and Parsons.—*Ed.*)

Part II: The Schutz-Parsons Letters

1. Talcott Parsons "On building social system theory: a personal history," *Daedalus*, 1970, 826–81.

2. Helmut R. Wagner, Hobart College, is preparing a book-length biography of Alfred Schutz to be published soon. See also

his introduction to the anthology *Alfred Schutz: On Phenomenology and Social Relations* (Chicago: University of Chicago Press, 1970). For an extensive bibliography on "Schutzean Studies" see my contribution "Alfred Schütz" in: *Klassiker des soziologischen Denkens* (ed. Kaesler), vol. 2, Beck, Munich 1978.

Part III: Retrospect

1. Edited and authorized version of a letter (August 9, 1974) of Parsons to me. Only some duplications and personal remarks have been eliminated.

2. Charles S. Peirce, *Coll. Pap.* 5.428–29, 8.191. In an earlier and implicit form see, for instance, the purport of "Man": 7.591.

3. The present-day dispute has been summarized by J. Cohen et al. in "De-Parsonizing Weber: The Critique of Parsons' Interpretation of Weber's Sociology," *American Sociological Review*, 40, 1975, 229–41. A commentary of Parsons, 666–70, and a rejoinder by the authors 670–74, appear in the same volume.

4. "Common-Sense and Scientific Interpretation of Human Action" (1953) and "Concept and Theory-Formation in the Social Sciences" (1954), *Coll. Pap.* 1. Comparing these studies with some of Talcott Parsons' *Essays in Sociological Theory* (New York: Free Press, 1954/1964), for instance with his 1945 paper on "Prospects of Systematic Theory," should show that Parsons and Schutz held to quite different notions of what is "empirical" and what is "concrete" in the sciences and everyday life.

5. Piet Tommissen, "Vilfredo Pareto," *Klassiker des soziologischen Denkens,* vol. 1, ed. Dirk Käsler (Munich: Beck, 1976), p. 227.

6. Max Weber, "Zur Geschichte der Handelsgesellschaften im Mittelalter," *Gesammelte Aufsätze zur Sozial- und Wirtschaftsgeschichte* (Tübingen: Mohr, 1924), 312–443.

7. For the notion of "epistemic claim," see Aron Gurwitsch, *Phenomenology and the Theory of Science,* ed. L. Embree (Evanston, Ill.: Northwestern University Press, 1966), p. 148. (The term was coined by Richard Zaner.) The "epistemic claim of sociology to the world of everyday life" is, of course, no specific phenomenological claim. Erving Goffman, for instance, and Henri Lefèbvre share the same claim, but from very different methodological positions. See E. Goffman, *The Presentation of Self in Everyday Life* (New York: Doubleday, 1959), and his more recent *Frame*

Analysis (New York: Harper and Row, 1974); H. Lefèbvre, *La vie quotidienne dans le monde moderne* (Paris, 1968).

8. For a recent discussion of Weber's position, see Constans Seyfarth, "Struktur und Reichweite 'handlungstheoretischer' Ansätze: Das Beispiel Max Webers," *Proceedings of 18. Deutscher Soziologentag Bielefeld 1976* (Stuttgart: Enke, forthcoming); for Parsons' position, see Enno Schwanenberg, *Soziales Handeln—Die Theorie und ihr Problem* (Bern: Huber, 1970); for Schutz's, see Richard Grathoff, "Ansätze zu einer Theorie sozialen Handelns bei Alfred Schutz," in *Neue Hefte für Philosophie,* 9, 1976, 115–33.

9. John von Neumann and Oskar Morgenstern, *Theory of Games and Economic Behavior* (Princeton, N. J.: Princeton University Press, 1944). I would like to draw attention to their discussion of "The Problem of Rational Behavior" (pp. 8–17) and its significance for studies of measurement in everyday life (p. 20).

10. A single example, simple and charming in its explicit recognition of the limitation of these approaches, must stand for a vast literature in this field: Y. Murakami, *Logic and Social Choice* (London: Routledge and Kegan Paul, 1968). See especially the chapters "Democracy in a World of Two Alternatives" (pp. 28–51) and "Welfare Economics" (pp. 130ff.).

11. See p. 37, this volume.

12. See note 3 of the introduction.

13. Parsons' retrospect, pp. 117 and 123.

14. For Parsons, see "Values, Motives, and Systems of Action," in *Toward a General Theory of Action.* For Schutz, see his *Reflections on the Problem of Relevance,* ed. Richard Zaner (New Haven: Yale University Press, 1970). See also the posthumous publication of Alfred Schutz and Thomas Luckmann, *The Structures of the Life-World* (Evanston: Northwestern University Press, 1973). An intermediate course is taken by Harold Garfinkel, who wrote his dissertation with Talcott Parsons but was also thoroughly acquainted with the work of Alfred Schutz. See his *Studies in Ethnomethodology* (Englewood Cliffs, N. J.: Prentice-Hall, 1967). Unfortunately, his dissertation, "The Perception of the Other: A Study in Social Order" (Harvard, 1952), is still not available to the general public.

15. This circumscribes the literal meaning of Schutz's *Der sinnhafte Aufbau der sozialen Welt,* a meaningful and constructive framing and reframing of the social world—through social action.

The Schutzean theme has found widest elaboration in Peter Berger's and Thomas Luckmann's *The Social Construction of Reality* (New York: Doubleday, 1966).

16. Letter from Alfred Schutz to Aron Gurwitsch, April 26, 1941 (my trans.). A publication of this correspondence is in preparation.

INDEX

Subject Index

Name Index
(Excluding Parsons and Schutz)